> MENUS

Order with ease and tuck in with pleasure – foreign language menus will never be an indecipherable mystery again.

> A PACKED SCHEDULE

Do you want culture, adventure, theatre, diving trips, or language and cooking classes? We've got phrases to make your trip even more exciting.

> LOCAL KNOWLEDGE

Insider Tips To help you pass for an insider, not just a tourist.

DOS AND DON'TS!
Help you to avoid faux pas.

WARNING! SLANG
Understand the locals better!

The colours, patterns and materials below are handy for shopping trips.
You'll find more help for (almost!) every situation throughout this book.

PRONUNCIATION

To make life easier, we've included a simple pronunciation guide after all the German words and phrases in this book. Just pronounce most of the sounds exactly as you would if you were reading them in English.

There are a few sounds in German that English speakers don't say very often (if at all). But don't worry – just bear the following notes in mind as you go along and you'll be sounding like a local in no time:

kh – we've used this letter combination to represent the hard German 'ch' sound you'll hear in words like *das Buch* [dass bookh] ("book"). It's pronounced in the back of the throat like the 'ch' in the Scottish word "**Loch**" (i.e. Loch Ness).

ei – the German 'ei' sound is pronounced like the English word "**eye**" (e.g. opinion: *die Meinung* [dee mei-nung]).

ow – in this book, say this sound as in the English words "**how**" and "**now**" (and not "below").

zj and **añ/oñ** – German has a number of words borrowed from French (*das Restaurant* [dass ress-toh-rañ]; *die Orange* [dee oh-rañ-zjuh]). When you see **zj**, say the sound of the "**g**" in the English word "**massage**". The letter combinations **añ** and **oñ** represent French nasal sounds – say "**an**" and "**on**" as you would normally, but don't let your tongue touch the roof of your mouth.

e – when you see a single letter 'e' written in the pronunciation guide (e.g. hotel: *das Hotel* [dass hoh-tel]), pronounce it with a flat sound – a bit like the 'e' in the English word "**bed**".

hyphens - hyphens have been used to make the pronunciation guide easier to read. All the sounds connected by hyphens should be joined together when you say them out loud.

Whenever you see a word split up – e.g. **Rind(~fleisch), (Edel~)Stein** – either say the part of the word outside the brackets on its own, or join the two halves together. The choice is yours!

GENDERS

German nouns come in three genders – masculine, feminine and neuter. There are two ways to tell the gender of a word in this book: either look for the abbreviations m = masculine, f = feminine, and nt = neuter, or keep an eye out for the tell-tale German words for "a/an" and "the".

You'll see "**the**" in three forms before nouns on their own: **der** (masculine), **die** (feminine), and **das** (neuter). Plural nouns always take **die**, no matter what gender they are in the singular form. You'll come across "**a/an**" in three main forms: **ein** (masculine and neuter), **einen** (masculine) and **eine** (feminine).

Note: the German words for "a/an" and "the" change depending on their context in a sentence. But with nouns written on their own in a list, you'll always be able to rely on spotting the forms mentioned above.

German has three words for 'you': '**Sie**', '**du**' and '**ihr**'. '**Sie**' is used in formal situations and with people you don't know very well. When you get to know someone better, use '**du**'. If you're talking to more than one person in a casual setting, use '**ihr**'.

ABBREVIATIONS

adj	adjective	s.o.	someone	pl	plural
adv	adverb	m	masculine	inf	informal
n	noun	f	feminine	etw	etwas = something
v	verb	nt	neuter	jdn/jdm	jemanden/jemandem =
sth	something	sing	singular		someone

Note: there is no distinction between adjectives and adverbs in German – one word serves both purposes (gut = good *and* well).

> SEA VIEWS AND EXTRA BEDS

Whether you want a dreamy seaside hotel or an extra bed in your room: arrange it all by email, by fax or over the phone and you can go on holiday relaxed in the knowledge that everything's sorted out.

BOOKING BY EMAIL

HOTEL | HOTEL [hoh-tel]

Dear Sir/Madam,
I would like to reserve a (single/double/twin) bedroom for (two) nights from the (28th) to the (30th) of June. I would be grateful if you could send me confirmation of this reservation and let me know the price for the two nights including breakfast. Many thanks in advance. Best wishes,

PLANNING YOUR TRIP

Sehr geehrte Damen und Herren,
am (28.) und (29.) Juni benötige ich für (zwei) Nächte ein (Einzel~/Doppel~/
Zweibett~)Zimmer. Bitte teilen Sie mir mit, ob Sie ein Zimmer frei haben und
was es pro Nacht (einschließlich Frühstück) kostet.
Mit freundlichen Grüßen,

■■RENTAL CARS | MIETWAGEN [meet-vahgen]■

Dear Sir/Madam,
I would like to rent a small car/midrange car/minivan from Frankfurt airport from the (20th)

to the (27th) of July. I would like to return the car to Munich airport, as my return flight leaves from there. Could you please send me your prices and let me know which documents I will require?
Best wishes,

Sehr geehrte Damen und Herren,
für den Zeitraum vom (20.) bis (27.) Juli möchte ich ab Flughafen Frankfurt einen Kleinwagen/Mittelklassewagen/Minivan mieten. Ich fliege vom Flughafen München ab und möchte den Leihwagen deshalb dort abgeben. Bitte schicken Sie mir eine Preisliste und teilen Sie mir mit, welche Unterlagen ich benötige.
Mit freundlichen Grüßen,

ACCOMMODATION ENQUIRIES

I'm looking for a nice hotel/bed and breakfast (with good food) in the old town.
Ich suche ein schönes Hotel/Bed and Breakfast in der Altstadt (mit besonders guter Küche).
[ish zookhuh ein sherness hoh-tel/bet ant brekfesst in dair alt-shtat [mit bezonderss gooter kuu-shuh]]

Is it central/quiet/near the beach?
Ist es zentral/ruhig/in Strandnähe gelegen?
[isst ess tsen-trahl/roo-ish/in shtrant-nayuh ge-laygen]

How much does it cost per week?
Wie viel kostet das pro Woche?
[vee feel kosstet dass proh vokh-uh]

Is there a website or an email address for this accommodation?
Hat diese Unterkunft eine Internet- oder E-Mail-Adresse? [hat deezuh unter-kunft einuh internet ohder ee-mayl-adressuh]

hotel	das Hotel [dass hoh-tel]
guest house	die Pension [dee penzee-ohn]
(bed)room	das Zimmer [dass tsim-er]
holiday apartment	die Ferienwohnung [dee fairee-en-vohnung]

HOTEL/GUEST HOUSE/ROOMS
HOTEL/PENSION/ZIMMER [hoh-tel/penzee-ohn/tsim-er]

Where to Stay: page 68

I'd like to stay in a hotel, but nothing too expensive – something mid-priced.
Ich suche ein Hotel, jedoch nicht zu teuer – etwas in der mittleren Preislage. [ish zookhuh ein hoh-tel, yay-dokh nisht tsoo toyer et-vass in dair mit-len preiss-lah-guh]

PLANNING YOUR TRIP

I'm looking for a hotel with...	Ich suche ein Hotel mit ... [ish zookhuh ein hoh-tel mit]
a swimming pool.	einem Swimmingpool. [einem svim-ing-pool]
a golf course.	einem Golfplatz. [einem golf-plats]
tennis courts.	Tennisplätzen. [teniss-pletsen]
Can you give me a quiet room/ a room with a view/ a room with a balcony?	Können Sie mir ein ruhiges Zimmer/ Zimmer mit Aussicht/Zimmer mit Balkon geben? [kernen zee meer ein roo-igess tsim-er/tsim-er mit owss-zisht/ tsim-er mit bal-kohn gayben]
Is it possible to put an extra bed in the room?	Ist es möglich, ein weiteres Bett im Zimmer aufzustellen? [isst ess merk-lish, ein veiter-ess bet im tsim-er owf-tsoo-shtel-en]

HOLIDAY HOMES/HOLIDAY APARTMENTS
FERIENHÄUSER/FERIENWOHNUNGEN [fairee-en-hoyzer/fairee-en-vohnungen]

 Where to Stay: page 74

I'm looking for a self-catering flat or bungalow.	Ich suche eine Ferienwohnung oder einen Bungalow. [ish zookhuh einuh fairee-en-vohnung ohder einen bungaloh]
Is there...?	Gibt es ...? [geept ess]
a kitchen	eine Küche [einuh kuu-shuh]
a dishwasher	eine Spülmaschine [einuh shpuul-masheenuh]
a refrigerator	einen Kühlschrank [einen kuul-shrank]
a washing machine	eine Waschmaschine [einuh vash-masheenuh]
a TV	einen Fernseher [einen fairn-zayr]
Wi-Fi	WLAN [vay-lahn]
Is electricity included in the price?	Sind die Stromkosten im Preis enthalten? [zint dee shtrohm-kosten im preiss ent-halten]
Are bed linen and towels provided?	Werden Bettwäsche und Handtücher gestellt? [vairden bet-veshuh unt hant-tuusher ge-shtelt]
How much deposit do you require and how long in advance?	Wie viel muss ich anzahlen und wann ist die Anzahlung fällig? [vee feel muss ish an-tsahlen unt van isst dee an-tsahlung fel-ish]
Where and when should I pick up the keys?	Wo und wann kann ich die Schlüssel abholen? [voh unt van kan ish dee shluussel ap-hohlen]

CAMPING | CAMPING [kemping]

I'm looking for a campsite (on the waterfront).	Ich suche einen schönen Campingplatz (am Wasser). [ish zookhuh einen shernen kemping-plats (am vasser)]
Is there anything you can recommend?	Können Sie mir irgendetwas empfehlen? [kernen zee meer irgent et-vass emp-faylen]

> EXPERIENCE MORE

Don't be shy! Whether it's small talk in a café, chatting away on a shopping trip or flirting in a club – just get stuck in! It's easier than you think and a great way to spice up your trip!

■ SAYING HELLO | BEGRÜSSUNG [be-gruu-sung]

Good morning!	Guten Morgen! [gooten morgen]
Good afternoon!	Guten Tag! [gooten tahk]
Good evening!	Guten Abend! [gooten ahbent]
Hello!	Hallo!/Grüß dich! [haloh/gruuss dish]
How are you?	Wie geht es Ihnen/dir? [vee gayt ess eenen/deer]
And you?	Und Ihnen/dir? [unt eenen/deer]

BASIC CONVERSATION

What's your name?	Wie ist Ihr Name?/Wie heißt du? [vee isst eer nahmuh/vee heisst doo]
Nice to meet you!	Nett, Sie/dich kennenzulernen! [net, zee/dish kenen-tsoo-lairnen]
May I introduce you?	Darf ich bekannt machen? [darf ish bekant makhen]
This is...	Das ist ... [dass isst]
Ms X./Mr X.	Frau X./Herr X. [frow X/hair X]
my partner.	mein Partner m./meine Partnerin f. [mein part-ner/meinuh part-ner-in]

GOODBYE/BYE! | AUF WIEDERSEHEN! [owf veeder-zayen]

Bye!	Tschüss! [tshuuss]
See you later!/See you soon!	Bis später! [biss shpayter]/Bis bald! [biss balt]
See you tomorrow!	Bis morgen! [biss morgen]
Good night!	Gute Nacht! [gootuh nakht]
It was nice to meet you.	Es war schön, Sie/dich kennenzulernen.
	[ess var shern, zee/dish kenen-tsoo-lairnen]

PLEASE | BITTE [bituh]

Could you do me a favour?	Darf ich Sie um einen Gefallen bitten?
	[darf ish zee um einen ge-fal-en bit-en]
Can you help me, please?	Können Sie mir bitte helfen? [kernen zee meer bituh helfen]
May I?	Gestatten Sie? [ge-shtat-en zee]
Don't mention it.	Bitte sehr. [bituh zair]
You're welcome.	Gern geschehen. [gairn ge-shayen]
With pleasure!	Mit Vergnügen! [mit fairg-nuugen]

THANK YOU! | DANKE [dankuh]

Thank you very much!	Vielen Dank. [feelen dank]
Yes, thank you!	Danke, sehr gern. [dankuh, zair gairn]
No, thank you!	Nein, danke. [nein, dankuh]
Thank you. The same to you!	Danke, gleichfalls! [dankuh, gleish-falss]
That's very kind, thank you.	Das ist nett, danke. [dass isst net, dankuh]

I'M SORRY!
ENTSCHULDIGUNG! [entshuldigung]

I'm sorry (I'm late)!	Tut mir leid(, dass ich zu spät komme)!
	[toot meer leit(, dass ish tsoo shpayt kom-uh]]
What a pity!	Schade! [shah-duh]

ALL THE BEST! | ALLES GUTE! [aless gootuh]

Congratulations!	Herzlichen Glückwunsch! [hairts-lish-en gluuk-vunsh]
Happy birthday!	Alles Gute zum Geburtstag! [aless gootuh tsum ge-burts-tahk]
Good luck!	Viel Erfolg!/Viel Glück!/Hals- und Beinbruch!
	[feel airfolk/feel gluuk/halss unt bein-brukh]

BASIC CONVERSATION

■ COMPLIMENTS | KOMPLIMENTE [komplee-mentuh]

How nice/lovely!	Wie schön! [vee shern]
That's wonderful/great!	Das ist wunderbar! [dass isst vunderbar]
You speak very good English.	Sie sprechen sehr gut Englisch. [zee shpre-shen zair goot en-glish]
You're looking well!	Sie sehen gut aus! [zee zayen goot owss]
I think you're very nice.	Ich finde Sie sehr sympathisch/nett.
	[ish finduh zee zair zuum-pah-tish/net]

beautiful	schön [shern]
excellent	ausgezeichnet [owss-ge-tseish-net]
friendly	freundlich [froynt-lish]
impressive	beeindruckend [buh-ein-druk-ent]
marvelous	herrlich [hair-lish]
nice	angenehm [an-ge-naym]
pleasant	nett [net]
pretty	hübsch [huupsh]
tasty	lecker [lek-er]

■ SMALL TALK | SMALLTALK [smorl-tork]

PERSONAL INFORMATION ZUR PERSON [tsoor pair-zohn]

What do you do for a living?	Was machen Sie/machst du beruflich?
	[vass makhen zee/makhsst doo be-roof-lish]
I'm a...	Ich bin ... [ish bin]
I work for...	Ich arbeite bei ... [ish arbeituh bei]
I'm still at school.	Ich gehe noch zur Schule. [ish gayuh nokh tsoor shooluh]

LOCAL KNOWLEDGE

moin moin

Insider Tip

You had me at Hello...

You can often tell where a German speaker is from as soon as they open their mouths. That's because the way people say 'hi' varies greatly from region to region. You can spot people from the north of Germany, for example, because they'll often say *moin* [moyn] or *moin moin* [moyn moyn] when they see each other. In contrast, natives of the south of Germany and Austria commonly greet each other with a hearty *Grüß Gott* [gruuss got] ("God greets (you)") or *Servus* [sairvuss] ("At your service"). You can tell if someone is from Switzerland by listening out for the Swiss-German *Grüezi* [gruu-tsee].

I'm a student.	Ich bin Student/in m/f. [ish bin shtoo-dent/in]
How old are you?	Wie alt sind Sie? polite/pl [vee alt zint zee]/
	Wie alt bist du inf/sing? [vee alt bisst doo]
I'm (twenty-four).	Ich bin (vierundzwanzig).
	[ish bin (feer-unt-svant-sish)]

ORIGIN AND STAY HERKUNFT UND AUFENTHALT [hairkunft unt owf-ent-halt]

Where do you come from?	Woher kommen Sie/kommst du?
	[voh-hair kom-en zee/komsst doo]
I'm from (London).	Ich komme aus (London).
	[ish kom-uh owss (lon-don)]
I'm from England.	Ich komme aus England.
	[ish kom-uh owss en-glant]
Have you been here long?	Sind Sie/Bist du schon lange hier?
	[zint zee/bisst doo shohn languh heer]
I've been here since...	Ich bin seit … hier. [ish bin zeit … heer]
How long are you staying?	Wie lange bleiben Sie/bleibst du?
	[vee languh blei-ben zee/bleipsst doo]
Do you like it?	Wie finden Sie es? [vee finden zee ess]
What's your e-mail address?	Wie ist Ihre/deine E-Mail-Adresse?
	[vee isst eeruh/deinuh eemayl-adressuh]

HOBBIES HOBBYS [hobeess]

What do you do in your spare time?	Was machen Sie/machst du in der Freizeit?
	[vass makhen zee/makhsst doo in dair freit-seit]
I'm interested in art/culture/ architecture/fashion.	Ich interessiere mich für … [ish interess-eeruh mish fuur]
	Kunst [kunsst]/Kultur [kultoor]/
	Architektur [arsh-ee-tek-toor]/Mode. [moh-duh]
Are you on Facebook?	Sind Sie/bist du auf Facebook?
	[zint zee/bisst doo owf fayssbuk]

cards/board games	Karten/Brettspiele [karten/bret-shpeeluh]
cinema/movies	das Kino [dass keenoh], Filme m [filmuh]
computer games	Computerspiele [kompyooter-shpeeluh]
cooking	kochen [kokhen]
learning languages	Sprachen lernen [shprah-khen lairnen]
listening to music	Musik f hören [moozeek hur-ren]
making music	Musik f machen [moozeek makhen]
meeting friends	Freunde m treffen [froynduh tref-en]
painting	malen [mahlen]
reading	lesen [layzen]
taking photos	fotografieren [foh-toh-graf-eer-en]
travelling	reisen [reizen]

BASIC CONVERSATION

SPORT SPORT [shport]

 A Packed Schedule: page 84

What sports do you do?	Welchen Sport treiben Sie/treibst du?
	[velshen shport treiben zee/treipsst doo]
I play football/tennis/ volleyball/handball/ table tennis.	Ich spiele … [ish speeluh] Fußball [fooss-bal]/Tennis [teniss]/ Volleyball [volay-bal]/Handball [hant-bal]/ Tischtennis. [tish-teniss]
I go to the gym/to yoga regularly.	Ich gehe regelmäßig ins Fitnesscenter/zum Yoga.
	[ish gayuh raygel-may-sish inss fit-ness-tsenter/tsum yohgah]
I go jogging/swimming/ cycling.	Ich jogge/schwimme/fahre Rad.
	[ish jog-uh/shvimuh/fah-ruh raht]

■ MAKING A DATE | VERABREDUNG/FLIRT [fair apray-dung/flert] ■

Have you got any plans for tomorrow?	Haben Sie/Hast du morgen schon etwas vor?
	[hahben zee/hasst doo morgen shohn et-vass for]
Shall we meet up this evening?	Treffen wir uns heute Abend? [tref-en veer unss hoytuh ahbent]
When/Where shall we meet?	Wann/Wo treffen wir uns? [van/voh tref-en veer unss]
Can I take you home?	Darf ich Sie/dich nach Hause bringen? [darf ish zee/dish nahk howzuh bringen]
Have you got a boyfriend/a girlfriend?	Hast du einen Freund/eine Freundin?
	[hasst doo einen froynt/einuh froyn-din]
Are you married?	Sind Sie verheiratet? [zint zee fair-hei-rah-tet]
I've been looking forward to seeing you all day.	Ich habe mich den ganzen Tag auf dich gefreut.
	[ish hahbuh mish dayn gan-tsen tahk owf dish ge-froyt]
You've got beautiful eyes!	Du hast wunderschöne Augen!
	[doo hasst vunder-shernuh ow-gen]
I've fallen in love with you.	Ich habe mich in dich verliebt.
	[ish hahbuh mish in dish fair-leept]
I love you!	Ich liebe dich! [ish leebuh dish]
I love you, too.	Ich liebe dich auch. [ish leebuh dish owkh]
I would like to sleep with you.	Ich möchte mit dir schlafen. [ish mershtuh mit deer shlah-fen]
But only if we use a condom!	Aber nur mit Kondom! [ahber noor mit kon-dohm]
Do you have condoms?	Hast du Kondome? [hasst doo kon-doh-muh]
Where can I buy some?	Wo kann ich welche kaufen? [voh kan ish velshuh kowfen]
I don't want to.	Ich will nicht. [ish vil nisht]
Please leave now!	Bitte geh jetzt! [bituh gay yetst]
Stop immediately!	Hör sofort auf! [hur zoh-fort owf]
Go away/Get lost!	Hau ab! [how ap]
Please leave me alone!	Lassen Sie/Lass mich bitte in Ruhe!
	[lass-en zee/lass mish bituh in roo-uh]

TIME

■TIME | UHRZEIT [oor-tseit]

WHAT TIME IS IT? WIE VIEL UHR IST ES? [vee feel oor isst ess]

 Time: Inside front cover

WHAT TIME?/WHEN? UM WIE VIEL UHR?/WANN? [um vee feel oor/van]

At (one) o'clock.	Um (ein) Uhr. [um (ein) oor]
In an hour's time.	In einer Stunde. [in einer shtunduh]
Between (three) and (four).	Zwischen (drei) und (vier). [tsvish-en (drei) unt (feer)]

HOW LONG? WIE LANGE? [vee languh]

Two hours.	Zwei Stunden (lang). [tsvei shtun-den (lang)]
From (ten) to (eleven).	Von (zehn) bis (elf). [fon (tsayn) biss (elf)]
Till (five) o'clock.	Bis (fünf) Uhr. [biss (fuunf) oor]

SINCE WHEN? SEIT WANN? [zeit van]

Since (eight am).	Seit (acht) Uhr (morgens). [zeit (akht) oor (morgenss)]
For half an hour.	Seit einer halben Stunde. [zeit einer halben shtun-duh]

■OTHER EXPRESSIONS OF TIME
■SONSTIGE ZEITANGABEN [zonss-tiguh tseit-an-gah-ben]

in the morning	morgens [morgenss]
during the morning	vormittags [for-mit-ahkss]
at lunchtime	mittags [mit-ahkss]
in the afternoon/evening	nachmittags [nahkh-mit-ahkss]/abends [ahbents]
at night	nachts [nakh-ts]
the day before yesterday	vorgestern [for-gesstern]
yesterday	gestern [gesstern]
ten minutes ago	vor zehn Minuten [for tsayn meenooten]
today/tomorrow	heute [hoytuh]/morgen [morgen]
now	jetzt [yet-st]
the day after tomorrow	übermorgen [uuber-morgen]
this week	diese Woche [deezuh vokhuh]
at the weekend	am Wochenende [am vokhen-enduh]
on Sunday	am Sonntag [am zon-tahk]
in a fortnight's time	in vierzehn Tagen [in feert-sayn tahgen]
next year	nächstes Jahr [nayk-stess yar]

BASIC CONVERSATION

sometimes	manchmal [mansh-mahl]
every half hour	alle halbe Stunde [aluh halbuh shtun-duh]
every hour	stündlich [shtuunt-lish]
every day	täglich [tayk-lish]
every other day	alle zwei Tage [aluh tsvei tahguh]
within a week	innerhalb einer Woche [inerhalp einer vokhuh]
soon	bald [balt]

■ THE DATE | DATUM [dahtum]

What's the date (today)?	Den Wievielten haben wir (heute)?
	[dayn vee-feel-ten hahben veer (hoytuh)]
Today's the first of May.	Heute ist der erste Mai. [hoytuh isst dair air-stuh mei]

■ DAYS OF THE WEEK | WOCHENTAGE [vokhen-tahguh]

Monday	Montag [mohn-tahk]
Tuesday	Dienstag [deenss-tahk]
Wednesday	Mittwoch [mit-vokh]
Thursday	Donnerstag [don-erss-tahk]
Friday	Freitag [frei-tahk]
Saturday	Samstag [zamss-tahk]
Sunday	Sonntag [zon-tahk]

LOCAL KNOWLEDGE

Insider Tips

▶ Time Flies.

Warning: if a German speaker tells you to meet them somewhere at *halb zehn* [halp tsayn] (lit: "half ten") don't trust your instincts! It actually means "half to ten": if you arrive at 10.30, you'll be a whole hour late. The same goes for *dreiviertel vier* [drei-firtel-feer] (lit: "three-quarters four"). It's not 4:45, as you might expect – it's actually three quarters of the way to four, or 3:45.

▶ Don't be Late!

People in the German-speaking world tend to place great importance on punctuality. You'll sometimes hear people apologising for their tardiness at times you might consider perfectly acceptable. And if you invite someone for dinner at your place at 7.30, then be prepared for them to arrive on the door when the clock strikes – and not a casual 15 or 20 minutes later, as you might expect them to at home.

MONTHS OF THE YEAR | MONATE [mohn-atuh]

January	Januar [yanoo-ar]
February	Februar [fay-broo-ar]
March	März [mairts]
April	April [a-pril]
May	Mai [mei]
June	Juni [yoo-nee]
July	Juli [yoo-lee]
August	August [ow-gusst]
September	September [zep-tember]
October	Oktober [ok-tohber]
November	November [noh-vember]
December	Dezember [day-tsember]

SEASONS | JAHRESZEITEN [yahress-tsei-ten]

spring	Frühling [fruu-ling]
summer	Sommer [zom-er]
autumn/fall	Herbst [hair-psst]
winter	Winter [vinter]

HOLIDAYS | FEIERTAGE [fei-er-tah-guh]

New Year's Day	Neujahr [noy-yar]
Epiphany	Heilige drei Könige [hei-li-guh drei kern-iguh]
Maundy Thursday	Gründonnerstag [gruun-don-erss-tahk]
Good Friday	Karfreitag [kar-frei-tahk]
Easter/Easter Monday	Ostern [oh-stern]/Ostermontag [oh-ster-mohn-tahk]
Labour Day (1st of May)	Tag der Arbeit [tahk dair arbeit]
Ascension	Christi Himmelfahrt [krisstee him-el-fart]
Pentecost	Pfingsten [pfing-sten]
The Feast of Corpus Christi	Fronleichnam [frohn-leish-nahm]
National Holiday (3rd of Oct)	Nationalfeiertag [natsee-ohn-ahl-fei-er-tahk]
Assumption Day	Mariä Himmelfahrt [maree-er him-el-fart]
All Saints' Day (1st of Nov)	Allerheiligen [al-er-hei-ligen]
All Souls' Day (2nd of Nov)	Allerseelen [al-er-zaylen]
Immaculate Conception (8th of Dec)	Mariä Empfängnis [maree-er emp-feng-niss]
Christmas Eve	Heiligabend [heiligahbent]
Christmas	Weihnachten [vei-nakh-ten]
New Year's Eve	Silvester [zilvesster]

THE WEATHER

What's the weather going to be like today?	Wie wird das Wetter heute? [vee virt dass vet-er hoytuh]
It's going to stay fine/remain poor.	Es bleibt schön/schlecht. [ess bleipt shern/shlesht]
It's going to get warmer/colder.	Es wird wärmer/kälter. [ess virt vairmer/kelter]
It's going to rain/snow.	Es soll regnen/schneien. [ess zol rayg-nen/shnei-en]
It's cold/hot/close.	Es ist kalt/heiß/schwül. [ess isst kalt/heiss/shvuul]
What's the temperature today?	Wie viel Grad haben wir heute? [vee feel graht hahben veer hoytuh]
It's (20) degrees.	Es hat (zwanzig) Grad Celsius. [ess hat (tsvant-sish) graht tsel-zee-uss]

air	die Luft [dee luft]
changeable	wechselhaft [vekssel-haft]
climate	das Klima [dass kleemah]
close/muggy/oppressive	schwül [shvuul]
cloud	die Wolke [dee volkuh]
cloudy	bewölkt [be-verlkt]
cold	kalt [kalt]
drought	die Trockenheit [dee trok-en-heit]
flood	die Überschwemmung [dee uuber-shvem-ung]
fog	der Nebel [dair naybel]
frost	der Frost [dair frosst]
heat	die Hitze [dee hit-suh]
high tide	die Flut [dee floot]
(very) hot	(sehr) heiß [(zair) heiss]
lightning	der Blitz [dair blits]
low tide	die Ebbe [dee eb-uh]
rain	der Regen [dair raygen]
rainy	regnerisch [rayg-ner-ish]
snow	der Schnee [dair shnay]
sun	die Sonne [dee zon-uh]
sunny	sonnig [zon-ish]
temperature	die Temperatur [dee temperatoor]
thunder	der Donner [dair don-er]
thunderstorm	das Gewitter [dass ge-vit-er]
warm	warm [varm]
wet	nass [nass]
wind	der Wind [dair vint]

> WHICH WAY TO THE...?

If you're lost, confused, or simply don't know where to go:
ask someone! This chapter will help you get back on track.

HOW DO I GET TO...?

Excuse me, where's..., please?	Entschuldigung, wo ist ...? [entshuldigung, voh isst]
Excuse me, how do you get to...?	Können Sie mir sagen, wie ich nach ... komme? [kernen zee meer zah-gen, vee ish nahkh ... komuh]
What's the quickest way to...?	Welches ist der kürzeste Weg nach/zu ...? [velshess isst dair kuur-tsess-tuh vayk nahkh/tsoo]
How far is it?	Wie weit ist es? [vee veit isst ess]
How far is it to...?	Wie weit ist es zum/zur ...? [vee veit isst ess tsum/tsoor]

OUT AND ABOUT

It's a long way away.	Es ist weit. [ess isst veit]
It isn't far.	Es ist nicht weit. [ess isst nisht veit]
Go straight on.	Gehen Sie geradeaus. [gayen zee ge-rah-duh owss]
Turn left/right.	Gehen Sie nach links/rechts.
	[gayen zee nahkh linkss/reshts]
The first/second street on the left/right.	Die erste/zweite Straße links/rechts.
	[dee airsstuh/tsveituh shtrah-suh linkss/reshts]
Cross... the bridge/ the square/the street.	Überqueren Sie … die Brücke/den Platz/die Straße.
	[uuber-kvairen zee … dee bruukuh/dayn plats/dee shtrah-suh]
Then ask again.	Dann fragen Sie noch einmal.
	[dan frahgen zee nokh einmahl]

You can take...	Sie können … nehmen. [zee kern ... naymen]
the bus.	den Bus [dayn buss]
the tram.	die Straßenbahn [dee shtrah-sen-bahn]
the tube (the underground).	die U-Bahn [dee oo-bahn]

AT THE BORDER

■ CUSTOMS/PASSPORT | ZOLL/REISEPASS [reize-pass]

Your passport, please!	Ihren Pass, bitte! [eeren pass, bituh]
Your passport has expired.	Ihr Pass ist abgelaufen. [eer pass isst ap-ge-low-fen]
Have you got a visa?	Haben Sie ein Visum? [hahben zee ein veezum]
Can I get a visa here?	Kann ich das Visum hier bekommen? [kan ish dass veezum heer be-kom-en]
Have you got anything to declare?	Haben Sie etwas zu verzollen? [hahben zee et-vass tsoo fair-tsol-en]
Pull over to the right, please.	Fahren Sie bitte rechts ran. [fahren zee bituh reshts ran]
Open the boot (trunk)/ this case, please.	Öffnen Sie bitte den Kofferraum/diesen Koffer. [erfnen zee bituh dayn kof-er-rowm/deezen kof-er]
Do I have to pay duty on this?	Muss ich das verzollen? [muss ish dass fair-tsol-en]
No, I've only got a few presents (gifts).	Nein, ich habe nur ein paar Geschenke. [nein, ish hahbuh noor ein par ge-shen-kuh]

Christian name, first name	der Vorname [dair for-nahm-uh]
customs	Zoll m [tsol]
date of birth	das Geburtsdatum [dass ge-boorts-dahtum]
driving licence	der Führerschein [dair fuurer-shein]
duty-free	zollfrei [tsol-frei]
enter the country	einreisen [ein-reizen]
export	die Ausfuhr [dee owss-foor]
ID card	de Personalausweis [pair-zohn-ahl-owss-veiss]
import	die Einfuhr [dee ein-foor]
leave the country	ausreisen [owss-reizen]
liable to customs duty	zollpflichtig [tsol-pflish-tish]
maiden name	der Geburtsname [dair ge-boorts-nahmuh]
marital status	der Familienstand [dair fameelee-en-stant]
married	verheiratet [fair-hei-rah-tet]
nationality	die Staatsangehörigkeit [dee shtahts-an-ge-her-rish-keit]
passport	der Reisepass [dair reize-pass]

place of birth	der Geburtsort [dair ge-boorts-ort]
place of residence	der Wohnort [dair vohn-ort]
single	ledig [lay-dish]
surname	der Nachname [dair nahkh-nah-muh]
valid	gültig [guul-tish]
visa	das Visum [dass veezum]

TRAVELLING BY CAR/MOTORBIKE/BICYCLE

HOW DO I GET TO...? | WIE KOMME ICH NACH ...? [vee komuh ish nahkh]

How far is it?	Wie weit ist das? [vee veit isst dass]
Excuse me, is this the road to...?	Entschuldigung, ist das die Straße nach ...? [entshuldigung, isst dass dee shtrah-suh nahkh]
How do I get to the motorway to...?	Wie komme ich zur Autobahn nach ...? [vee komuh ish tsoor ow-toh-bahn nahkh]
Straight on until you get to... Then turn left/right.	Immer geradeaus bis ... Dann links/rechts abbiegen. [im-er ge-rah-duh owss biss ... dan linkss/reshts ap-bee-gen]

FILL UP THE TANK, PLEASE | VOLLTANKEN, BITTE [fol-tanken, bituh]

Where's the nearest petrol/ gas station, please?	Wo ist bitte die nächste Tankstelle? [voh isst bituh dee naykss-tuh tank-shteluh]
95 octane/98 octane/ diesel/charging point for electric vehicles	Normalbenzin [normahl-ben-tseen]/Super [zooper]/ Diesel [dee-zel]/Elektroladestation [aylek-troh-la-duh-shat-see-ohn]
Please check the oil/the tyre/tire pressure.	Prüfen Sie bitte den Ölstand/den Reifendruck. [pruufen zee bituh dayn erl-shtant/dayn rei-fen-druk]
Where are the toilets, please?	Wo sind bitte die Toiletten? [voh zint bituh dee twa-let-en]

■PARKING | PARKEN [parken]

Is there somewhere to park near here?
Gibt es hier in der Nähe eine Parkmöglichkeit?
[geept ess heer in dair nayuh einuh park-merk-lish-keit]

Can I park my car here?
Kann ich mein Auto hier abstellen?
[kan ish mein owtoh heer ap-shtel-en]

■BREAKDOWN | PANNE [pan-uh]

Could you help me jump-start my car?
Können Sie mir Starthilfe geben?
[kernen zee meer shtart-hil-fuh gayben]

Would you send a mechanic/ a breakdown truck, please?
Würden Sie mir bitte einen Mechaniker/ einen Abschleppwagen schicken? [vuurden zee meer bituh einen may-shah-niker/einen ap-shlep-vahgen shik-en]

Could you give me some petrol/gas, please?
Könnten Sie mir mit Benzin aushelfen?
[kernten zee meer mit ben-tseen owss-helfen]

Could you help me change the tyre/tire, please?
Könnten Sie mir beim Reifenwechsel helfen?
[kernten zee meer beim reifen-vekssel helfen]

Could you give me a lift to the nearest garage/ petrol (gas) station?
Würden Sie mich bis zur nächsten Werkstatt/ Tankstelle mitnehmen? [vuurden zee mish biss tsoor naykss-ten vairk-shtat/tank-shteluh mit-naymen]

■GARAGE | WERKSTATT [vairk-shtat]

The car won't start.
Mein Wagen springt nicht an.
[mein vahgen shpringt nisht an]

Could you have a look?
Können Sie mal nachsehen?
[kernen zee mahl nahkh-zayen]

The battery is flat.
Die Batterie ist leer.
[dee bat-air-ee isst lair]

There's something wrong with the engine.
Mit dem Motor stimmt was nicht.
[mit daym moh-tor shtimt vass nisht]

The brakes don't work.
Die Bremsen funktionieren nicht.
[dee bremzen funk-tsee-oh-nee-ren nisht]

...is/are faulty.
… ist/sind defekt. [isst/zint dayfekt]

I'm losing oil.
Der Wagen verliert Öl.
[dair vahgen fair-leert erl]

Change the sparkplugs, please.
Wechseln Sie bitte die Zündkerzen aus.
[vek-seln zee bituh dee tsuunt-kairt-sen owss]

How much will it cost?
Was wird es kosten?
[vass virt ess kossten]

OUT AND ABOUT

■ ACCIDENT | UNFALL [un-fal]

Please call...	Rufen Sie bitte … [roofen zee bituh]
an ambulance.	einen Krankenwagen. [einen kranken-vahgen]
the police.	die Polizei. [dee poh-lee-tsei]
the fire-brigade.	die Feuerwehr. [dee foyer-vair]
Are you injured?	Sind Sie verletzt? [zint zee fair-letst]
Have you got a first-aid kit?	Haben Sie Verbandszeug? [hahben zee fair-bants-tsoyk]
It was my fault.	Es war meine Schuld. [ess var meinuh shult]
It was your fault.	Es war Ihre Schuld. [ess var eeruh shult]
Shall we call the police, or can we settle things ourselves?	Sollen wir die Polizei holen oder können wir uns so einigen? [zol-en veer dee poh-lee-tsei hohlen ohder kernen veer unss zoh ein-igen]
I'd like my insurance company to take care of the damage.	Ich möchte den Schaden durch meine Versicherung regeln lassen. [ish mershtuh dayn shah-den doorsh meinuh fair-zish-erung raygeln lass-en]
Please give me your name and address.	Geben Sie mir bitte Ihren Namen und Ihre Anschrift. [gayben zee meer bituh eeren nahmen unt eeruh an-shrift]
Thank you very much for your help.	Vielen Dank für Ihre Hilfe. [feelen dank fuur eeruh hilfuh]

accelerator	das Gaspedal [dass gahss-pay-dahl]
alcohol level	Promille [proh-mi-luh]
(automatic) transmission	das (Automatik~)Getriebe [dass (ow-toh-mah-tik~)ge-treebuh]
backfire	die Fehlzündung [dee fayl-tsuun-dung]
battery	die Batterie [dee bat-air-ee]
bell	die Klingel [dee klingel]
bend (in a road, etc.)	die Kurve [dee kur-vuh]
bicycle, bike	das Fahrrad [dass far-raht]
brake pad	der Bremsbelag [dair bremss-be-lahk]
breakdown	die Panne [dee panuh]
breakdown service	der Pannendienst [dair pan-en-deensst]
broken	gebrochen [ge-bro-khen]
cable	das Kabel [dass kah-bel]
car park (parking lot)	der Parkplatz [dair park-plats]
car wash	die Autowäsche [dee owtoh-veshuh]
carburettor	der Vergaser [dair fair-gahzer]
clutch	die Kupplung [dee kup-lung]
coolant	das Kühlwasser [dass kuul-vasser]
country road	die Landstraße [dee lant-shtrah-suh]
crash helmet	der Helm [dair helm]
crossroads, junction	die Kreuzung [dee kroy-tsung]
diversion/detour	die Umleitung [dee um-leit-ung]
driving licence	der Führerschein [dair fuurer-shein]

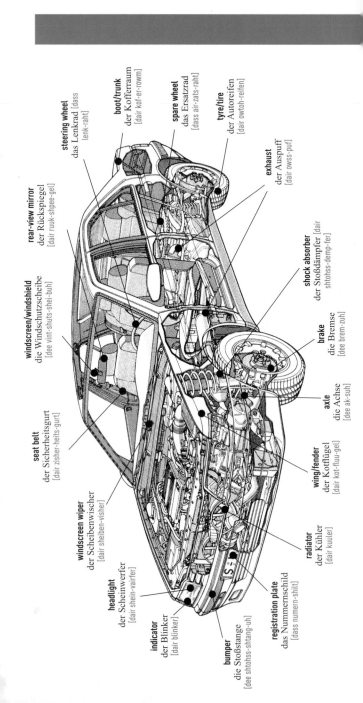

steering wheel
das Lenkrad [dass
lenk-raht]

boot/trunk
der Kofferraum
[dair kof-er-rowm]

spare wheel
das Ersatzrad
[dass air-zats-raht]

tyre/tire
der Autoreifen
[dair owtoh-reifen]

rear-view mirror
der Rückspiegel
[dair ruuk-shpee-gel]

exhaust
der Auspuff
[dair owss-puf]

windscreen/windshield
die Windschutzscheibe
[dee vint-shuts-shei-buh]

shock absorber
der Stoßdämpfer [dair
shtohss-demp-fer]

brake
die Bremse
[dee brem-zuh]

seat belt
der Sicherheitsgurt
[dair zisher-heits-gurt]

axle
die Achse
[dee ak-suh]

windscreen wiper
der Scheibenwischer
[dair sheiben-visher]

wing/fender
der Kotflügel
[dair kot-fluu-gel]

headlight
der Scheinwerfer
[dair shein-vairfer]

radiator
der Kühler
[dair kuuler]

indicator
der Blinker
[dair blinker]

registration plate
das Nummernschild
[dass numern-shilt]

bumper
die Stoßstange
[dee shtohss-shtang-uh]

dynamo/alternator	die Lichtmaschine [dee lisht-masheenuh]
emergency telephone	die Notrufsäule [dee noht-roof-zoyluh]
fan belt	der Keilriemen [dair keil-reemen]
fault n	der Defekt [dair dayfekt]
fine	das Bußgeld [dass booss-gelt]
flat tyre (tire)/puncture	die Reifenpanne [dee reifen-pan-uh]
footbrake	die Fußbremse [dee fooss-brem-zuh]
fuel station for electric cars	die Elektrotankstelle [dee aylek-troh-tank-shteluh]
full/high beam lights	das Fernlicht [dass fairn-lisht]
fully comprehensive insurance	die Vollkaskoversicherung [dee fol-kassk-oh-fair-zish-erung]
garage	die Werkstatt [dee vairk-shtat]
gear	der Gang/die Gangschaltung [dair gang/dee gang-shaltung]
gearbox	das Getriebe [dass ge-tree-buh]
green card (insurance)	die grüne Versicherungskarte [dee gruunuh fair-zish-er-ungss-kartuh]
handbrake	die Handbremse [dee hant-bremzuh]
hazard warning light	der Warnblinker [dair varn-blinker]
heating	die Heizung [dee hei-tsung]
hitch-hiker	der Tramper/die Tramperin [dair tremper/dee tremper-in]
horn	die Hupe [dee hoopuh]
horsepower; hp	die Pferdestärke; PS [dee pfair-de-shtair-kuh; pay-ess]
ignition	die Zündung [dee tsuun-dung]
ignition key	der Zündschlüssel [dair tsuunt-shluuss-el]
ignition switch	das Zündschloss [dass tsuunt-shloss]
jack	der Wagenheber [dair vahgen-hayber]
jump lead	das Starthilfekabel [dass shtart-hilfe-kahbel]
lane	die Fahrspur [dee far-shpoor]
lorry, truck	der Lastwagen [dair lasst-vahgen]
motor, engine	der Motor [dair moh-tor]
motorway/highway	die Autobahn [dee owtoh-bahn]
motorway service station (rest stop)	die Raststätte [dee rasst-shtet-uh]
mudguard	das Schutzblech [dass shuts-blesh]
multi-storey car park/ parking lot	das Parkhaus [dass park-howss]
natural gas (LPG) station	die Erdgastankstelle [dee airt-gahss-tank-shteluh]
octane number	die Oktanzahl [dee ok-tahn-tsahl]
oil, oil change	das Öl [dass erl], der Ölwechsel [dair erl-vek-sel]
papers (documents)	Papiere nt [papeeruh]
petrol/gas	Benzin nt [ben-tseen]
petrol/gas can	der Benzinkanister [dair ben-tseen-kann-isster]
petrol/gas station	die Tankstelle [dee tank-shteluh]
pump	die Luftpumpe [dee luft-pumpuh]
rack	der Gepäckträger [dair ge-pek-trayger]

radar speed check	die Radarkontrolle [dee ra-dar-kontroluh]
(puncture) repair kit	das Flickzeug [dass flik-tsoyk]
rim	die Felge [dee fel-guh]
road map	die Straßenkarte [dee shtrah-sen-kartuh]
road works	die Baustelle [dee bow-shtel-uh]
roof rack	der Dachgepäckträger [dair dakh-ge-pek-trayger]
scooter	der Motorroller [dair moh-tor-rol-er]
screw	die Schraube [dee shrow-buh]
sidelights	das Standlicht [dass shtant-lisht]
sign	das Straßenschild [dass shtra-sen-shilt],
	der Wegweiser [dair vayk-veizer]
spanner, wrench	der Schraubenschlüssel [dair shrow-ben-shluussel]
spark plug	die Zündkerze [dee tsuunt-kairt-suh]
speedometer	der Tachometer [dair takh-oh-mayter]
starter	der Anlasser [dair an-lasser]
street, road	die Straße [dee shtrah-suh]
sunroof	das Schiebedach [dass shee-be-dakh]
toll (charge)	die Maut [dee mowt]
tool	das Werkzeug [dass vairk-tsoyk]
tow (away)	abschleppen [ap-shlep-en]
towrope	das Abschleppseil [dass ap-shlep-zeil]
traffic jam	der Stau [dair shtow]
traffic lights	die Ampel [dee ampel]
valve	das Ventil [dass vent-eel]
warning triangle	das Warndreieck [dass varn-drei-ek]
wheel brace	der Radmutterschlüssel [dair raht-mut-er-shluussel]

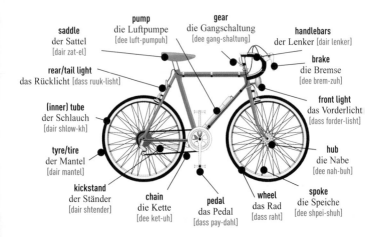

pump
die Luftpumpe [dee luft-pumpuh]

gear
die Gangschaltung [dee gang-shaltung]

saddle
der Sattel [dair zat-el]

handlebars
der Lenker [dair lenker]

brake
die Bremse [dee brem-zuh]

rear/tail light
das Rücklicht [dass ruuk-lisht]

front light
das Vorderlicht [dass forder-lisht]

(inner) tube
der Schlauch [dair shlow-kh]

hub
die Nabe [dee nah-buh]

tyre/tire
der Mantel [dair mantel]

kickstand
der Ständer [dair shtender]

chain
die Kette [dee ket-uh]

pedal
das Pedal [dass pay-dahl]

wheel
das Rad [dass raht]

spoke
die Speiche [dee shpei-shuh]

OUT AND ABOUT

CAR/MOTORBIKE/BICYCLE HIRE
AUTO-/MOTORRAD-/FAHRRADVERMIETUNG

I'd like to hire...	Ich möchte für (zwei) Tage/(eine) Woche … mieten.
for (2) days/for (a week).	[ish mershtuh fuur (tsvei) tahguh/(einuh) vokhuh … meeten]
a car/a camper van/	ein Auto/ein Wohnmobil/einen Roller/ein Fahrrad
a scooter/a bicycle	[ein owtoh/ein vohn-mohbeel/einen rol-er/ein far-raht]
I'd like an automatic/	Bitte mit Automatik/Klimaanlage/
air-conditioning/	Navigationsgerät. [bituh mit owtoh-mah-tik/kleemah anlah-guh/
a navigation system.	navee-ga-tsee-ohnss-ge-rayt]
How much does it cost	Wie hoch ist die Tages-/Wochenpauschale?
per day/week?	[vee hoh-kh isst dee tahgess-/vokhen-pow-shah-luh]
What do you charge	Wie viel verlangen Sie pro gefahrenem km?
per km?	[vee feel fair-langen zee proh ge-fahren-em kah-em]
Does the vehicle have	Ist das Fahrzeug vollkaskoversichert?
comprehensive insurance?	[isst dass far-tsoyk fol-kass-koh-fair-zish-ert]
Is it possible to return	Ist es möglich, das Fahrzeug in … abzugeben?
the car in/at...?	[isst ess merklish, dass fart-soyk in … ap-tsoo-gay-ben]

TRAVELLING BY PLANE

DEPARTURE | ABFLUG [ap-flook]

Where's the counter for	Wo ist der Schalter von …?
(name of airline)?	[voh isst dair shalter fon]
When's the next flight to...?	Wann fliegt die nächste Maschine nach …?
	[van fleekt dee naykss-tuh mashee-nuh nahkh]
I'd like to book a single/	Ich möchte einen einfachen Flug/
return flight to...	Hin- und Rückflug nach … buchen.
	[ish mershtuh einen ein-fakhen flook/hin unt ruuk-flook
	nahkh … bookhen]
Are there still seats	Sind noch Plätze frei?
available?	[zint nokh pletsuh frei]
I'd like to cancel this flight.	Ich möchte diesen Flug stornieren.
	[ish mershtuh deezen flook shtor-neeren]
I'd like to change the booking.	Ich möchte diesen Flug umbuchen.
	[ish mershtuh deezen flook um-bookhen]

Can I take this on as hand luggage/baggage?	Kann ich das als Handgepäck mitnehmen? [kan ish dass alss hant-ge-pek mit-naymen]
Is the plane to... late?	Hat die Maschine nach ... Verspätung? [hat dee masheenuh nahkh ... fair-shpay-tung]

■ ARRIVAL | ANKUNFT [an-kunft]

My luggage/baggage is missing.	Mein Gepäck ist verloren gegangen. [mein ge-pek isst fair-lor-en ge-gangen]
My suitcase has been damaged.	Mein Koffer ist beschädigt worden. [mein kof-er isst be-shay-disht vorden]

airline	die Fluggesellschaft [dee flook-ge-zel-shaft]
airport bus	der Flughafenbus [dair flook-hahfen-buss]
airport tax	die Flughafengebühr [dee flook-hahfen-ge-buur]
boarding card	die Bordkarte [dee bort-kartuh]
booking	die Buchung [dee bookh-ung]
cancel	stornieren [shtor-neeren]
change (a booking)	umbuchen [um-bookhen]
check in v	einchecken [ein-chek-en]
connection	der Anschluss [dair an-shluss]
counter	der Schalter [dair shalter]
delay	die Verspätung [dee fair-shpay-tung]
departure	der Abflug [dair ap-flook]
direct flight	der Direktflug [dair dee-rekt-flook]
duty-free shop	der zollfreie Laden [dair tsol-frei-uh lahden]
e-ticket	das elektronische Ticket [dass ay-lek-troh-nish-uh tik-et]
emergency exit	der Notausgang [dair noht-owss-gang]
emergency landing	die Notlandung [dee noht-landung]
flight	der Flug [dair flook]
hand luggage/baggage	das Handgepäck [dass hant-ge-pek]
landing	die Landung [dee landung]
life jacket	die Schwimmweste [dee shvim-vesstuh]
luggage/baggage	das Gepäck [dass ge-pek]
luggage/baggage claim	die Gepäckkontrolle [dee ge-pek-kontrol-uh]
on board	an Bord [an bort]
online booking	die Internetbuchung [dee internet-bookhung]
pilot	der Pilot [dair pee-loht], die Pilotin [dee pee-loht-in]
plane	das Flugzeug [dass flook-tsoyk]
route	die Flugstrecke [dee flook-shtrek-uh]
scheduled time of departure	der planmäßige Abflug [dair plahn-may-sig-uh ap-flook]

security control	die Sicherheitskontrolle [dee zisher-heits-kontrol-uh]
sick bag	die Spucktüte [dee shpuk-tuutuh]
steward/	der Flugbegleiter [dair flook-be-gleiter]/
stewardess	die Flugbegleiterin [dee flook-be-gleiter-in]
stopover	die Zwischenlandung [dee tsvishen-landung]
time of arrival	die Ankunftszeit [dee an-kunfts-tseit]
timetable	der Flugplan [dair flook-plahn]
window seat	der Fenstersitz [dair fensster-zits]

TRAVELLING BY TRAIN

■ AT THE STATION | AM BAHNHOF [am bahn-hohf]

When's the next train to...?	Wann fährt der nächste Zug nach ...? [van fairt dair naykss-tuh tsook nahkh]
A second-class/first-class single to..., please.	Eine einfache Fahrt zweiter/erster Klasse nach ..., bitte. [einuh ein-fakhuh fart tsveiter/airsst-uh klass-uh nahkh ..., bituh]
Two returns to..., please.	Zweimal ... hin und zurück, bitte. [tsvei-mahl ... hin unt tsoo-ruuk, bituh]
Is there an economy fare?	Gibt es einen Spartarif? [geept ess einen shpar-tareef]
Is there a reduction for children/students?	Gibt es eine Ermäßigung für Kinder/Studenten? [geept ess einuh air-may-si-gung fuur kinder/shtoo-dent-en]
Do I have to reserve a seat?	Muss ich einen Platz reservieren? [muss ish einen plats rayzair-veeren]
I'd like to register this suitcase.	Ich möchte diesen Koffer als Reisegepäck aufgeben. [ish mershtuh deezen kof-er alss reize-ge-pek owf-gayben]
Is the train from... running late?	Hat der Zug aus ... Verspätung? [hat dair tsook owss ... fair-shpay-tung]
(Where) Do I have to change?	(Wo) Muss ich umsteigen? [(voh) muss ish um-shtei-gen]
Which platform/track does the train for... leave from?	Von welchem Gleis fährt der Zug nach ... ab? [fon velshem gleiss fairt dair tsook nahkh ... ap]
Can I take a bicycle?	Kann ich ein Fahrrad mitnehmen? [kan ish ein far-raht mit-naymen]

■ ON THE TRAIN | IM ZUG [im tsook]

Excuse me, is this seat free?	Verzeihung, ist dieser Platz noch frei? [fair-tsei-ung, isst deezer plats nokh frei]
Does this train stop in...?	Hält dieser Zug in ...? [helt deezer tsook in]

arrive v	ankommen [an-kom-en]
Child's ticket	die Kinderfahrkarte [dee kinder-far-kartuh]
compartment	das Abteil [dass ap-teil]
connecting train	der Anschlusszug [dair an-shluss-tsook]
departure,	die Abfahrt [dee ap-fart],
time of departure	die Abfahrtszeit [dee ap-farts-tseit]
emergency brake	die Notbremse [dee noht-brem-zuh]
engaged	besetzt [be-zet-st]
express train	der Intercity [dair inter-sit-ee]
fare	der Fahrpreis [dair far-preiss]
free/vacant	frei [frei]
get on	einsteigen [ein-shtei-gen]
get out	aussteigen [owss-shtei-gen]
Internet booking,	die Internetbuchung [dee internet-bookhung],
printout	der Ausdruck [dair owss-druk]
left-luggage/baggage locker	das Schließfach [dass shleess-fakh]
left-luggage/baggage office	die Gepäckaufbewahrung [dee ge-pek owf-be-vahrung]
left-luggage/baggage ticket	der Gepäckschein [dair ge-pek-shein]
luggage/baggage	das Gepäck [dass ge-pek]
main station	der Hauptbahnhof [dair howpt-bahn-hohf]
motorail service	der Autoreisezug [dair owtoh-reize-tsook]
platform/track	der Bahnsteig/das Gleis [dair bahn-shteik/dass gleiss]
power socket	der Stromanschluss [dair shtrohm an-shluss]
reduction	die Ermäßigung [dee air-may-si-gung]
restaurant/dining car	der Speisewagen [dair shpeize-vahgen]
return ticket	die Rückfahrkarte [dee ruuk-far-kartuh]
seat reservation	die Sitzplatzreservierung [dee zits-plats-rayzair-veerung]
sleeping car	der Schlafwagen [dair shlahf-vahgen]
station	der Bahnhof [dair bahn-hohf]
(station) stop	der Aufenthalt [dair owf-ent-halt]
supplement	der Zuschlag [dair tsoo-shlahk]
taken	besetzt [be-zet-st]
ticket	die Fahrkarte [dee far-kartuh]
ticket office	der Fahrkartenschalter [dair far-karten-shalter]
timetable	der Fahrplan [dair far-plahn]
toilet	die Toilette [dee twa-let-uh]
train	der Zug [dair tsook]
train ferry	die Eisenbahnfähre [dee eizen-bahn-fayruh]
waiting room	die Wartehalle [dee vartuh-hal-uh]
window seat	der Fensterplatz [dair fensster-plats]

OUT AND ABOUT

TRAVELLING BY BOAT

AT THE PORT | AM HAFEN [am hah-fen]

When does the next ship leave for...?	Wann fährt das nächste Schiff/die nächste Fähre nach … ab? [van fairt dass naykss-tuh shif/dee naykss-tuh fayruh nahkk … ap]
How long does the crossing take?	Wie lange dauert die Überfahrt? [vee languh dow-ert dee uuber-fart]
I'd like a ticket to...	Ich möchte eine Fahrkarte nach … [ish mersh-tuh einuh far-kartuh nahkk]
I'd like a ticket for the round trip at... o'clock.	Ich möchte eine Karte für die Rundfahrt um … Uhr. [ish mersh-tuh einuh kartuh fuur dee runt-fart um … oor]
When do we arrive at...?	Wann legen wir in … an? [van laygen veer in … an]

ON BOARD | AN BORD [an bort]

Where's the restaurant/ lounge?	Wo ist der Speisesaal/der Aufenthaltsraum? [voh isst dair shpei-ze-zahl/dair owf-ent-halts-rowm]
I don't feel well.	Ich fühle mich nicht wohl. [ish fuuluh mish nisht vohl]
Could you give me something for seasickness, please.	Geben Sie mir bitte ein Mittel gegen Seekrankheit. [gayben zee meer bituh ein mit-el gaygen zay-krank-heit]

cabin	die Kabine [dee kabeenuh], die Kajüte [dee ka-yuu-tuh]
captain	der Kapitän [dair ka-pee-tayn]
car ferry/train ferry	die Autofähre/die Eisenbahnfähre [dee owtoh-fayruh/dee eizen-bahn-fayruh]
coast	die Küste [dee kuuss-tuh]
deck	das Deck [dass dek]
dock	der Anlegeplatz [dair an-lay-ge-plats]
excursion	der Landausflug [dair lant-owss-flook]
hovercraft	das Luftkissenboot [dass luft-kissen-boht]
life-jacket	die Schwimmweste [dee shvim-vesstuh]
lifebelt	der Rettungsring [dair retungss-ring]
lifeboat	das Rettungsboot [dass retungss-boht]
mainland	das Festland [dass fesst-lant]
motorboat	das Motorboot [dass moh-tor-boht]
on board	an Bord [an bort]
port	der Hafen [dair hah-fen]
rowing boat	das Ruderboot [dass rooder-boht]
rough seas	der Seegang [dair zay-gang]
seasick adj	seekrank [zay-krank]

steamer, steamship	der Dampfer [dair damp-fer]
Steward	der Steward [dair styoo-art]
ticket	die Fahrkarte [dee far-kartuh]
wave	die Welle [dee vel-uh]

PUBLIC TRANSPORT

▮ BUS/UNDERGROUND | BUS/U-BAHN [buss/oo-bahn] ▮

Excuse me,	Entschuldigung, wo ist die nächste …
	[entshuldigung, voh isst dee naykss-tuh]
where's the nearest...	
bus stop?	Bushaltestelle? [buss-halte-shteluh]
tram stop?	Straßenbahnhaltestelle? [shtrah-sen-bahn-halte-shteluh]
underground station?	U-Bahnstation? [oo-bahn-stat-see-ohn]
Which line goes to...?	Welche Linie fährt nach …? [velshuh leenee-uh fairt nahkh]
When does the bus leave?	Wann fährt der Bus ab? [van fairt dair buss ap]
Where do I have to get out/ change?	Wo muss ich aussteigen/umsteigen?
	[voh muss ish owss-shtei-gen/um-shtei-gen]
Will you tell me when we're there, please?	Sagen Sie mir bitte Bescheid, wenn ich aussteigen muss.
	[zah-gen zee meer bituh be-sheid, ven ish owss-shtei-gen muss]
Where can I buy a ticket?	Wo kann ich einen Fahrschein kaufen?
	[voh kan ish einen far-shein kow-fen]
A ticket to..., please.	Bitte einen Fahrschein nach …
	[bituh einen far-shein nahkh]
Can I take a bicycle?	Kann ich ein Fahrrad mitnehmen?
	[kan ish ein far-raht mit-nay-men]

bus	der Bus [dair buss]
buy a ticket	einen Fahrschein lösen
	[einen far-shein ler-zen]
departure	die Abfahrt [dee apfart]
driver	der Fahrer [dair fahrer]
fare	der Fahrpreis [dair far-preiss]
get on	einsteigen [ein-shtei-gen]
get out	aussteigen [owss-shtei-gen]
inspector	der Kontrolleur m [dair kontrol-uhr],
	die Kontrolleurin f [dee kontrol-uhr-in]
one-day travelcard	die Tageskarte [dee tah-gess-kartuh]
stop	die Haltestelle [dee halte-shteluh]
street, road	die Straße [dee shtrah-suh]
terminus	die Endstation [dee ent-shtat-see-ohn]
ticket	die Fahrkarte [dee far-kartuh]

ticket machine	der Fahrkartenautomat
	[dair far-karten owtoh-maht]
timetable	der Fahrplan [dair far-plahn]
tourist ticket	das Touristenticket [dass too-riss-ten-tik-et]
tram	die Straßenbahn [dee shtrah-sen-bahn]
underground	die U-Bahn [dee oo-bahn]
weekly season ticket	die Wochenkarte [dee vokhen-kartuh]

■ TAXI | TAXI [tak-see]

Would you call a taxi for me, please?	Könnten Sie mir bitte ein Taxi rufen?
	[kernten zee meer bituh ein tak-see roofen]
Where's the nearest taxi rank?	Wo ist der nächste Taxistand?
	[voh isst dair naykss-tuh tak-see-shtant]
To the station.	Zum Bahnhof. [tsum bahn-hohf]
To the... hotel.	Zum Hotel … [tsum hoh-tel]
To (name of street)	In die …-Straße. [in dee … shtrah-suh]
To..., please.	Nach …, bitte. [nahkh …, bituh]
How much will it cost to...?	Wie viel kostet es nach …? [vee feel koss-tet ess nahkh]
That's too much.	Das ist zu viel. [dass isst tsoo feel]
Could you stop here, please?	Halten Sie bitte hier. [halten zee bituh heer]
That's for you.	Das ist für Sie. [dass isst fuur zee]
I'd like a receipt, please.	Eine Quittung, bitte. [einuh kvit-ung, bituh]

fare	der Fahrpreis [dair far-preiss]
taxi driver	der Taxifahrer [dair tak-see-fah-rer]
taxi rank	der Taxistand [dair tak-see-shtant]
tip/gratuity	das Trinkgeld [dass trink-gelt]

LIFT SHARING

Are you going to...?	Fahren Sie nach …?
	[fahren zee nahkh]
Could you give me a lift to...?	Könnte ich bis … mitfahren?
	[kerntuh ish biss … mit-fahren]
I'd like to get out here.	Ich würde gerne hier aussteigen.
	[ish vuur-duh gairn-uh heer owss-shtei-gen]
Thank you very much for the lift.	Vielen Dank fürs Mitnehmen.
	[feelen dank fuurss mit-naymen]

>A CULINARY ADVENTURE

Order with ease and tuck in with pleasure – foreign menus will never be an indecipherable mystery again.

GOING FOR A MEAL | ESSEN GEHEN [essen gayen]

Is there... here?	Wo gibt es hier ... [voh geept ess heer]
a good restaurant	ein gutes Restaurant? [ein goo-tess ress-toh-rañ]
a restaurant serving local specialities	ein typisches Restaurant? [ein tuupish-ess ress-toh-rañ]
I would like to reserve a table for (four) for this evening, please.	Reservieren Sie uns bitte für heute Abend einen Tisch für (vier) Personen. [rayzairveeren zee unss bituh fuur hoytuh ahbent einen tish fuur (feer) pair-zohnen]
Is this table free?	Ist dieser Tisch noch frei? [isst deezer tish nokh frei]

FOOD & DRINK

A table for (two/three), please.	Einen Tisch für (zwei/drei) Personen, bitte.
	[einen tish fuur (tsvei/drei) pair-zohnen, bituh]
Do you have a (non)smoking area?	Haben Sie einen (Nicht~)Raucherbereich?
	[hahben zee einen (nisht~)rowkher-bereish]
Where are the toilets, please?	Wo sind bitte die Toiletten? [voh zint bituh dee twa-let-en]
Enjoy your meal!	Guten Appetit! [gooten apayteet]
Cheers!	Prost! [prohsst]
The food is/was great!	Das Essen ist/war ausgezeichnet!
	[dass essen isst/var owss-ge-tseish-net]
I'm full, thank you.	Ich bin satt, danke. [ish bin zat, dankuh]
Do you mind if I smoke?	Stört es Sie, wenn ich rauche? [shtert ess zee, ven ish rowkhuh]

Waiter, could I have...	Herr Ober, … [hair ohber]
the menu, please.	bitte die Speisekarte. [bituh dee shpeize-kartuh]
the drinks menu, please.	bitte die Getränkekarte. [bituh dee ge-trenkuh-kartuh]
What can you recommend?	Was können Sie mir empfehlen? [vass kernen zee meer emp-faylen]
I'll have...	Ich nehme … [ish naymuh]
I'm sorry but we've run	Wir haben leider kein/e … mehr.
out of...	[veer hahben leider kein/uh … mair]
I'd like to try a local speciality.	Ich hätte gerne etwas Typisches aus der Region.
	[ish het-uh gairnuh et-vass tuupish-ess owss dair ray-gee-ohn]
I'm a diabetic/vegetarian/	Ich bin Diabetiker/Vegetarier/Veganer.
vegan.	[ish bin dee-abay-teeker/vay-gay-tahr-ee-er/vay-gahner]
I'm allergic to... eggs/	Ich bin allergisch gegen … [ish bin alairgish gaygen]/Eier
gluten/dairy products/	[ei-er]/Gluten [gloo-tayn]/Milchprodukte [milsh-proh-duktuh]/
monosodium glutamate/nuts.	Natriumglutamat [nahtree-um-gloota-maht]/Nüsse [nuuss-uh].
What would you like to drink?	Was wollen Sie trinken? [vass vol-en zee trinken]
A glass of..., please.	Bitte ein Glas … [bituh ein glahss]
A bottle of/half a bottle	Bitte eine Flasche/eine halbe Flasche …
of..., please.	[bituh einuh flashuh/einuh halbuh flashuh]
Bring us..., please.	Bitte bringen Sie uns …, bitte. [bituh bringen zee unss …, bituh]

The food is cold.	Das Essen ist kalt. [dass essen isst kalt]
The meat has not been	Das Fleisch ist nicht durch. [dass fleish isst nisht doorsh]
cooked through.	
Have you forgotten my...?	Haben Sie mein/e … vergessen? [hahben zee mein/uh … fairgessen]
I didn't order that.	Das habe ich nicht bestellt. [dass hahbuh ish nisht beshtelt]
Fetch the manager, please.	Holen Sie bitte den Chef. [hohlen zee bituh dayn shef]

Could I have the bill/	Bezahlen, bitte. [be-tsahlen, bituh]
check, please?	
Everything on one	Bitte alles zusammen.
bill/check, please.	[bituh aless tsoo-zamen]
Could I have a receipt,	Könnte ich bitte eine Quittung bekommen?
please?	[kerntuh ish bituh einuh kvitung be-kom-en]
Separate bills/checks, please.	Getrennte Rechnungen, bitte. [ge-trentuh resh-nungen, bituh]
That's for you.	Das ist für Sie. [dass isst fuur zee]
Keep the change.	Es stimmt so. [ess shtimt zoh]

FOOD & DRINK

The food was excellent.	Das Essen war ausgezeichnet. [dass essen var owss-ge-tseish-net]
Thank you very much for the invitation!	Vielen Dank für die Einladung! [feelen dank fuur dee einlahdung]

boil v, cook v	kochen [kokhen]
bread	das Brot [dass broht]
breakfast	das Frühstück [dass fruu-shtuuk] > page 46
children's portion	der Kinderteller [dair kinder-tel-er]
cold	kalt [kalt]
cook (chef)	der Koch [dair kokh], die Köchin [dee ker-shin]
cup	die Tasse [dee tassuh]
cutlery, fork, knife, spoon	das Besteck [dass be-shtek], die Gabel [dee gahbel], das Messer [dass messer], der Löffel [dair ler-fel]

LOCAL KNOWLEDGE

Insider Tips

Come on in, the water's... fizzy.

Ordering normal tap water is usually frowned upon in restaurants, and if you ask for water in bars, you'll be given (and charged for!) fizzy *Mineralwasser* [mee-nair-al-vasser] by default.

Guten Appetit!

When you sit down to dine in the German-speaking world, don't tuck in straight away. The polite thing to do is to wait until everyone's served and then wish your fellow diners a *Guten Appetit* [gooten ap-ay-teet] ("Bon Appétit!"/Enjoy your meal) before starting.

Cheers!

Think before you take a drink! Before you dive in, you'll often be expected to say *Prost!* [prohsst] ("cheers") and clink glasses with everyone present first. If this sounds like a lot of work – it's not over yet! It's considered very bad luck not keep eye contact with your fellow imbibers when your glasses touch (a skill that can take practice!). The penalty for breaking this rule? A curse of seven bad years in the bedroom...

The Tipping Point

People often pay for what they've eaten separately – you'll be asked the question *Zusammen oder getrennt?* [tsoo-zam-en ohder ge-trent] ("together or separately"). If you're happy with the service, add 5–10% to the price of your meal. Hand your money over and say the amount you want to pay – if you don't want change, just say *Stimmt so!* [shtimt zo] ("keep the change!") or *Danke* [dankuh] ("thanks"). Tipping isn't necessary in Switzerland, where a service charge will usually be added to your bill.

deep-fried	frittiert [friteert]
dessert	der Nachtisch [dair nahkhtish] > page 50, 51
diabetic	der Diabetiker [dair dee-abay-teeker], die Diabetikerin [dee dee-abay-teeker-in]
dinner	das Abendessen [dass ahbent-essen]
dish of the day	das Tagesgericht [dass tahgess-ge-risht]
drink	das Getränk [dass ge-trenk] > page 45, 52, 53
fishbone	die Gräte [dee graytuh]
fresh	frisch [frish]
fried	gebacken [ge-bak-en]
garlic	der Knoblauch [dair knohb-low-kh]
glass	das Glas [dass glahss]
gluten-free	glutenfrei [gloo-tayn-frei]
gravy	die Soße [dee zohss-uh]
grilled	gegrillt [ge-grilt]
hot (spicy)	scharf [sharf]
(very) hot (temperature)	(sehr) heiß [(zair) heiss]
low-calorie	kalorienarm [kalohree-en-arm]
low-fat	fettarm [fet-arm]
lunch	das Mittagessen [dass mit-ahk-essen]
main course	die Hauptspeise [dee howpt-shpei-zuh] > page 48, 49
mustard	der Senf [dair zenf]
napkin	die Serviette [dee zairvee-etuh]
oil	das Öl [dass erl]
order n	die Bestellung [dee be-shtel-ung]
pepper	der Pfeffer [dair pfefer]
plate	der Teller [dair tel-er]
salt	Salz nt [zalts]
sauce	die Soße [dee zohss-uh]
seasoning	das Dressing [dass dressing]
soup	die Suppe [dee zup-uh] > page 47
sour	sauer [zow-er]
spice	das Gewürz [dass ge-vuurts]
starter	die Vorspeise [dee for-shpeizuh] > page 46
sugar, (without) sugar	Zucker m [tsu-ker], (ohne) Zucker m [(ohnuh) tsu-ker]
sweet	süß [zuuss]
tip/gratuity	das Trinkgeld [dass trink-gelt]
toothpick	der Zahnstocher [dair tsahn-shtokh-er]
vegetarian	vegetarisch [vay-gay-tah-rish]
vinegar	der Essig [dair essish]
waiter, waitress	der Kellner [dair kelner], die Kellnerin [dee kelner-in]
water	das Wasser [dass vasser]
wholemeal	Vollkorn nt [fol-korn]

der Salat
[dair zalaht]

Bohnen f
[bohnen]

die Peperoni
[dee pay-pair-oh-nee]

Paprika m/f
[papree-kah]

Tomaten f
[toh-mahten]

die Gurke
[dee gurkuh]

der Blumenkohl
[dair bloomen-kohl]

der Brokkoli
[dair brok-oh-lee]

Artischocken f
[artee-shok-en]

Champignons m
[shañ-peen-yoñ]

die Aubergine
[dee ohbair-zjeen-uh]

der Sellerie
[dair zeleree]

Kartoffeln f
[karto-feln]

die Zwiebel
[dee tsvee-bel]

der Knoblauch
[dair knohb-lowkh]

der Ingwer
[dair ingver]

die Avocado
[dee avoh-kahdoh]

Karotten f [karot-en]
Möhren f [mer-en]

der Kohl
[dair kohl]

der Lauch
[dair lowkh]

der Spargel
[dair shpargel]

Linsen f
[linzen]

der Kürbis
[dair kuur-biss]

Zucchini m/f
[tsoo-kee-nee]

Erbsen f
[airp-sen]

Kichererbsen f
[kisher-airp-sen]

der Spinat
[dair shpee-naht]

der Mais
[dair meiss]

der Salbei
[dair zalbei]

die Minze
[dee mintsuh]

die Petersilie
[dee payter-zee-lee-uh]

der Rosmarin
[dair rohss-mareen]

Aprikosen f
[apree-kohzen]

Bananen f
[ban-ahn-en]

die Ananas
[dee an-an-ass]

Mango f
[mang-goh]

Erdbeeren f
[airt-bairen]

der Pfirsich
[dair pfir-zish]

die Kiwi
[dee kee-vee]

Weintrauben f
[vein-trowben]

der Apfel (pl Äpfel)
[dair apfel (epfel)]

Birnen f
[birnen]

Heidelbeeren f
[heidel-bairen]

Kirschen f
[kirshen]

Johannisbeeren f
[yoh-han-iss-bairen]

Orangen f
[oh-rañ-zjen]

die Zitrone
[dee tsee-trohnuh]

die Limette
[dee lee-met-uh]

die Papaya
[dee pap-ei-ah]

die Wassermelone
[dee vasser-maylohn-uh]

die Honigmelone
[dee hoh-nish-maylohn-uh]

die Grapefruit
[dee grayp-froot]

der Granatapfel
[dair granaht-apfel]

Pflaumen f
[pflowmen]

Mirabellen f
[meer-abel-en]

die Feige
[dee fei-guh]

Litschis f
[lit-sheess]

die Pampelmuse
[dee pampel-moozuh]

die Kokosnuss
[dee koh-koss-nuss]

Esskastanien f
[ess-kass-tah-nee-en]

Erdnüsse f
[airt-nuuss-uh]

Cranberries f
[krahn-bair-eez]

Trockenobst nt
[trok-en-oh-psst]

Studentenfutter nt
[shtoo-dent-en-fut-er]

das Brot/Toast m
[dass broht/tohsst]

das Schwarzbrot
[dass shvarts-broht]

das Vollkornbrot
[dass fol-korn-broht]

Baguette f/nt
[bag-et]

der Bagel
[dair bah-gel]

die Brezel
[dee bray-tsel]

das Croissant
[dass krwass-añ]

das Knäckebrot
[dass kne-ke-broht]

das Fladenbrot
[dass flah-den-broht]

das Brötchen
[dass brert-shen]

das Vollkornbrötchen
[dass fol-korn-brert-shen]

Pumpernickel m
[pumper-nikel]

die Waffel
[dee vafel]

der Donut
[dair doh-noot]

das Plundergebäck
[dass plunder-gebek]

der Kuchen
[dair kookhen]

die Reiswaffel
[dee reiss-vafel]

das Müsli
[dass muuss-lee]

Cornflakes
[korn-flaykss]

Jogurt m/nt
[yoh-goort]

die Butter
[dee but-er]

das Ei
[dass ei]

der Käse
[dair kayzuh]

der Blauschimmelkäse
[dair blow-shim-el-kayzuh]

der Camembert
[dair kam-om-bair]

der Frischkäse
[dair frish-kayzuh]

die Milch
[dee milsh]

der Kräuterquark
[dair kroyter-kvark]

der Bonbel
[dair boñ-bel]

der Parmesan
[dair parmay-zahn]

der Schafskäse
[dair shahfss-kayzuh]

das Rind
[dass rint]

Innereien m
[in-er-ei-en]

weiblich/männlich
[veip-lish/menlish]

das Kalb
[dass kalp]

das Schwein
[dass shvein]

das Lamm
[dass lam]

das Huhn
[dass hoon]

die Ente
[dee entuh]

der Hase
[dair hahzuh]

das Wildschwein
[dass vilt-shvein]

Fleisch nt **am Stück**
[fleish am shtuuk]

Fleisch nt **in Würfeln**
[fleish in vuurfeln]

Hackfleisch nt
[hak-fleish]

das/der Schaschlik
[dass/dair shash-lik]

das Steak
[dass stayk]

das Filet
[dass feelay]

das Kotelett
[dass kot-let]

das Roastbeef
[dass rohsst-beef]

das Würstchen
[dass vuursst-shen]

die Wurst
[dee vursst]

die Salami
[dee zalah-mee]

der gekochte Schinken
[dair ge-kokh-tuh shinken]

der rohe Schinken m
[dair roh-uh shinken]

der Speck
[dair shpek]

das Grillhähnchen
[dass gril-hayn-shen]

der Hähnchenschlegel
[dair hayn-shen-shlaygel]

der Wolfsbarsch
[dair volfss-barsh]

die Forelle
[dee foh-rel-uh]

der Thunfisch
[dair toon-fish]

der Lachs
[dair lakss]

Sardinen f
[zar-dee-nen]

Krabben f
[krab-en]

Scampi pl
[skam-pee]

der Hummer
[dair hum-er]

Muscheln f
[musheln]

Calamares m
[kala-mah-ress]

Austern f
[ow-stern]

der Kaviar
[dair kah-vee-ar]

**Mineralwasser nt
ohne Kohlensäure f**
[mee-ner-ahl-vasser
ohnuh kohlen-zoyruh]

**Mineralwasser nt
mit Kohlensäure f**
[mee-ner-ahl-vasser
mit kohlen-zoyruh]

die Milch
[dee milsh]

die Sojamilch
[dee zoh-yah-milsh]

der Saft
[dair zaft]

das/die Cola
[dass/dee koh-lah]

der Energydrink
[dair enair-jee-drink]

das Bier
[dass beer]

der Tee
[dair tay]

der Kaffee
[dair kaf-ay]

der Kakao
[dair kak-ow]

der Eiswürfel
[dair eiss-vuurfel]

der Rotwein
[dair roht-vein]

der Weißwein
[dair veiss-vein]

der Sekt
[dair zekt]

der Cocktail
[dair kok-tayl]

> Point & Show: page 43

Butter [but-er]	butter
harte/weiche Eier [hartuh/veishuh ei-er]	hard-boiled/soft-boiled eggs
Rührei [ruur-ei-er]	scrambled eggs
Honig [hohn-ish]**/Marmelade** [mar-me-lah-duh]	honey/jam
Kaffee [kafay], **Tee** [tay], **Milch** [milsh],	coffee, tea, milk,
Kakao [ka-kow], **Saft** [zaft]	cocoa, juice
Müsli [muuss-lee]	muesli
Obst [oh-psst]	fruit
Quark [kvark]	yoghurt-like soft cheese
Schinken [shin-ken]**/Käse** [kay-zuh]	ham/cheese
Wurstaufschnitt [vursst-owf-shnitt]	sliced sausages/salami
Brot/Brötchen/Toast [broht/brert-shen/tohsst]	bread/bread rolls/toast
Mehrkornbrot [mair-korn-broht]	multigrain bread (usually wheat/ rye/oats and sesame/linseed)
Roggenbrot [rog-en-broht]	dark rye bread
Sonnenblumenkernbrot [zon-en-bloo-men-kairn-broht]	rye bread with sunflower seeds
Vollkornbrot [fol-korn-broht]	whole grain bread

Bohnensalat [boh-nen-za-laht]	green bean and onion salad
Eiersalat [ei-er-za-laht]	egg with mayonnaise and mustard
Gemischter Salat [ge-mish-ter za-laht]	mixed salad
Handkäs mit Musik [hant-kayss mit moo-tseek]	sour milk cheese with vinegar and onions
Kartoffeln mit Grüner Soße [kar-tof-eln mit gruu-nuh zoh-suh]	boiled potatoes with a green sauce made with seven herbs
Krabbensalat [krab-en-za-laht]	prawn salad made with yoghurt, mayonnaise and cucumber
Obatzda [oh-bats-dah]	Bavarian delicacy made from cheese, butter, various spices and onions
Reibekuchen mit Lachs [rei-be-koo-khen mit lakss]	potato fritters with smoked salmon
Rollmops [rol-mopss]	pickled herrings rolled around onions, gherkins, olives, etc.
Spargel-Schinken-Röllchen [shpar-gel-shin-kel-rerl-shen]	asparagus and ham rolls
Wurstsalat [vursst-za-laht]	salad made with sausages, vinegar and onions

SUPPEN [zup-en] | SOUPS

Bärlauchsuppe [bayr-lowkh-zup-uh]	wild garlic and onion soup
Erbsensuppe [airp-sen-zup-uh]	thick pea soup
Fischbeuschelsuppe [fish-boy-shel-zup-uh]	fish, fish roe and vegetable soup
Frühlingssuppe [fruu-lingss-zup-uh]	spring vegetable soup
Graupensuppe [grow-pen-zup-uh]	barley (and vegetable) soup
Hühnersuppe mit Spargel [huuner-zup-uh mit shpargel]	chicken and vegetable broth with asparagus
Leberknödelsuppe [lay-ber-kner-del-zup-uh]	liver dumpling soup
Linsensuppe [lin-zen-zup-uh]	lentil soup

FISCH UND SCHALENTIERE [fish unt shahlen-teeruh] | FISH & SHELLFISH

> Point & Show: page 45

Aal [ahl]	eel
Austern [ow-stern]	oysters
Barsch [barsh]	perch
Forelle [foh-rel-uh]	trout
Garnelen [gar-nay-len]	prawns
Hering [hair-ing]	herring
Kabeljau [kah-bel-yow]	cod
Lachs [lakss]	salmon
Makrele [ma-kray-luh]	mackerel
Muscheln [mush-eln]	mussels
Scholle [shol-uh]	plaice
Thunfisch [toon-fish]	tuna
Tintenfisch [tinten-fish]	squid

FLEISCH/GEFLÜGEL [fleish/ge-fluu-gel] | MEAT/POULTRY

> Point & Show: page 44

Ente [en-tuh]	duck
Gans [ganss]	goose
Hackfleisch [hak-fleish]	mince
Hähnchen [hayn-shen]	chicken
Kalbfleisch [kalp-fleish]	veal
Keule [koy-luh]	leg
Mett [met]	seasoned pork, eaten raw
Rind(~fleisch) [rint(~fleish)]	beef

Rippe [rip-uh]	rib
Schinken [shin-ken]	ham
Schweinefleisch [shveinuh-fleish]	pork
Steak [stayk]	steak
Truthahn [troot-hahn]	turkey

■ WÜRSTE [vuurss-tuh] | SAUSAGES

Bockwurst [bok-vursst]	a Frankfurter, originally made with ground veal, now produced with a variety of different meats
Bratwurst [braht-vursst]	grilled/pan-fried sausage made from pork or beef, usually served with mustard and a bread roll
Currywurst [keree-vursst]	a Bratwurst served sliced and topped with curry powder and ketchup
Leberwurst [lay-ber-vursst]	spreadable liver sausage
Weisswurst [veiss-vursst]	white veal and bacon sausage, served with sweet mustard and soft pretzels

■ HAUPTSPEISEN [howpt-shpei-zen] | MAIN COURSES

Birnen, Bohnen und Speck [bir-nen, boh-nen unt shpek]	pears, beans and bacon, served with potatoes
Frikadelle [free-ka-del-uh]	large, flat meatballs
Gänsebraten [gen-ze-brah-ten]	roast goose
Himmel und Erde [him-el unt air-duh]	(lit: Heaven and Earth) sausages served with mashed potatoes and apple mousse
Jägerschnitzel [yay-ger-shnit-sel]	(lit: Hunter schnitzel) schnitzel served with mushroom sauce
Leberkäse [lay-ber-kay-zuh]	loaf-shaped sausage made from corned beef, pork, bacon and onions
Linsen mit Spätzle [linzen mit shpets-luh]	egg noodles and lentils, often served with sausages
Maultaschen [mowl-tashen]	pockets of pasta filled with meat and/or vegetables, often served in a broth
Rinderrouladen [rinder-roo-lah-den]	bacon, onions, mustard and pickles wrapped in thinly sliced beef
Sauerbraten [zow-er-brah-ten]	pot roast made with meat marinaded in vinegar or wine for several days, often served with red cabbage and egg noodles

Schweinebraten mit Rotkohl und Klößen
[shveinuh-brahten mit roht-kohl unt kler-sen]

roast pork with red cabbage and dumplings

Schweinshaxe [shveinss-hak-suh]

roast ham hock/pork knuckle, often served with potato dumplings and red cabbage

Spargel mit Sauce Hollandaise
[shpar-gel mit zoh-suh hol-on-dayz]

a seasonal dish of white asparagus, served with hollandaise sauce and boiled potatoes

Wiener Schnitzel [vee-ner shnit-sel]

a thin piece of veal in breadcrumbs (pork Schnitzels are often served as "Schnitzel Wiener Art" – Viennese-style schnitzels)

Zwiebelkuchen mit Federweißer
[tsvee-bel-kookhen mit fay-der-veisser]

tart topped with onions, bacon and sour cream, served with young, fizzy wine

BEILAGEN [bei-lah-gen] | SIDE ORDERS

Bratkartoffeln [braht-kar-tof-eln]

pan-fried potatoes

Kartoffelpüree [kar-tof-el-puu-ray]

mashed/puréed potato

Kartoffelpuffer/Reibekuchen
[kar-tof-el-puf-er /rei-buh-kookhen]

fried potato pancakes

Kartoffelsalat [kar-tof-el-za-laht]

potato salad

Knödel [kner-del]

dumplings made from potato and/or bread

Nudeln [noo-deln]

pasta/noodles

Spätzle [shpets-luh]

thick, short egg noodles, often served with various toppings (lentils, cheese, spices, etc.)

GEMÜSE [ge-muuzuh] | VEGETABLES

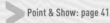

Point & Show: page 41

Blumenkohl [bloomen-kohl]

cauliflower

Bohnen [bohnen]

beans

Brokkoli [brok-oh-lee]

broccoli

Champignons [shañ-peen-yoñ]

button mushrooms

Erbsen [airpss-en]

peas

Grünkohl [gruun-kohl]

curly-leafed kale

Karotten/Möhren [ka-rot-en/mer-ren]

carrots

Kartoffeln [kar-tof-eln]

potatoes

Knoblauch [knoh-blowkh]

garlic

Kohl [kohl]

cabbage

Kohlrabi [kohl-rah-bee]	German turnip, can be eaten cooked or raw
Kürbis [kuur-biss]	pumpkin
Linsen [linzen]	lentils
Paprika [pap-ree-kah]	bell pepper
Pilze [pil-tsuh]	mushrooms
Rettich [retish]	radish; *Bier Rettich* is a long, white vegetable that's sliced thinly and served as a snack in beer gardens
Rotkohl [roht-kohl]	red cabbage in vinegar
Sauerkraut [zow-er-krowt]	finely cut, pickled cabbage
Zwiebeln [tsvee-beln]	onions

▮KÄSE [kayzuh] | CHEESE▮

> Point & Show: page 43

Bergkäse [bairk-kay-zuh]	(lit: mountain cheese) hard cheese with a strong, nutty flavour, produced in the Alps
Edamer [ay-dam-er]	spheres of wax-coated yellow cheese from Edam, Holland
Emmentaler [em-en-tah-ler]	yellow, medium-hard Swiss cheese
Frischkäse [frish-kay-zuh]	fromage frais/cream cheese
Handkäse [hant-kayzuh]	(lit: hand cheese) sour milk cheese from southern Hesse
Quark [kvark]	yoghurt-like soft cheese
Rauchkäse [rowkh-kay-zuh]	semi-soft smoked cheese with a brown, smoky rind
Weisslackerkäse/Bierkäse [veiss-lak-er-kay-zuh/beer-kay-zuh]	mild yet pungent cheese, often served with beer
Ziegenkäse [tseegen-kayzuh]	goat's milk cheese

▮KUCHEN & NACHTISCHE [kookhen unt nakh-tish-uh] | CAKES & DESSERTS▮

Armer Ritter [armer rit-er]	(lit: poor knight) French toast
Baumkuchen [bowm-kookhen]	(lit: tree cake) round, cylindrical cake, baked on a spit
Bayerische Creme [bei-er-ish-uh kraym]	a thick cream dessert flavoured with liqueur

Berliner [bair-leener]/ **Krapfen** [krap-fen]/ **Krepel** [kray-pel]	a jam-filled, sugar-dusted doughnut (warning: during certain festivals, a few may be filled with mustard to trick the unwary!)
Bienenstich [been-en-shtish]	vanilla custard, butter cream or cream on a layer of sweet dough, topped with caramelised almonds
Bratäpfel [braht-ep-fel]	baked apples with various sweet fillings, sometimes served with vanilla sauce
Dampfnudel [dampf-noo-deln]	a sweet roll served with vanilla sauce, jam or boiled fruit (can also be served as a savoury side dish)
Donauwelle [doh-now-vel-uh]	(lit: Danube wave) cake with a swirling pattern, made with sour cherries, butter cream, cocoa and chocolate
Kaiserschmarren [keizer-shmar-ren]	a shredded pancake served with various toppings (nuts, apples, cherries, plums, etc.)
Obstkuchen [oh-psst-kookhen]	cake filled with fruit
Rote Grütze [rohtuh gruu-tsuh]	red fruit pudding served with cream or vanilla sauce
Schwarzwälder Kirschtorte [shvarts-velder kirsh-tortuh]	Black Forest gateau – layers of chocolate cake with cherries and whipped cream
Wiener Apfelstrudel [vee-ner ap-fel-shtroo-del]	Viennese apple strudel – sweet apples encased in sugar-dusted puff pastry
Windbeutel [vint-boytel]	light profiteroles (cream puffs) filled with cream or vanilla sauce (and sometimes fruit)

BIER [beer] | BEER

Berliner Weiße [bair-leener veiss-uh]	white, cloudy beer from Berlin, often served in a large glass with raspberry or woodruff syrup
Bockbier [bok-beer]	strong, dark, malty lager
Dunkles/Helles Bier [dunk-less/hel-ess beer]	dark lager/pale ale
Kölsch [kerlsh]	a speciality beer from Cologne, sold in small, narrow glasses (200ml)
Pils/Pilsner [pilss/pilz-ner]	larger beer with a strong, hoppy flavour
(süßes/saueres) Radler [(zuuss-ess/zow-ress) rahd-ler]	(lit: (sweet/sour) cyclist) beer mixed with lemonade (süß = sweet) or fizzy water (sauer = sour)
Weißbier [veiss-beer], **Weizenbier** [vei-tsen-beer]	wheat beer

WEIN [vein] | WINE

Apfelwein [ap-fel-vein]	strong, tart apple wine
Champagner [sham-pan-yuh]	champagne
Eiswein [eiss-vein]	(lit: ice wine) sweet dessert wine made from grapes that have frozen while still on the vine
Federweißer [fay-der-veisser]	young, fizzy wine/fermented grape juice drunk from early September to late October
Glühwein [gluu-vein]	mulled wine – hot red wine mixed with fruit and spices
Rotwein/Weißwein/Rosé [roht-vein/veiss-vein/roh-zay]	red wine/white wine/rosé
trocken [trok-en]**/lieblich** [leep-lish]	dry/sweet
Sekt [zekt]	sparkling wine
Weinschorle [vein-shorluh]	wine spritzer

LIKÖR/SPIRITUOSEN [lee-kuhr/shpee-ree-too-oh-zen] | LIQUEURS/SPIRITS

Apfelkorn [ap-fel-korn]	sweet liqueur made with distilled apples
Eierlikör [ei-er-lee-kuhr]	an aperitif made from egg yolk, alcohol and sugar or honey
Jägermeister [yay-ger-meisster]	(lit: hunting master) liqueur made with a large number of herbs and spices
Kirsch(~wasser) [kirsh-vasser]	clear cherry brandy
Schnaps [shnapss]	strong, short drink, often made with distilled fruit

ALKOHOLFREIE GETRÄNKE [al-koh-hohl-frei-uh ge-tren-kuh]
SOFT DRINKS

Almdudler [alm-doodler]	Austrian soft drink made from apple and grape juice and various herbs
Apfelsaft [ap-fel-zaft]	apple juice
Apfelschorle [ap-fel-shorluh]	apple juice mixed with sparkling water
Eistee [eiss-tay]	ice tea
Limonade [lee-moh-nah-duh]	lemonade
Mineralwasser [mee-ner-ahl-vasser]	mineral water
Orangensaft [oh-rañ-zjen-zaft]	orange juice
Spezi [shpay-tsee]	cola mixed with orangeade
Traubensaft [trow-ben-zaft]	grape juice

THE DRINKS MENU

◼ WARME GETRÄNKE [varmuh ge-tren-kuh] | HOT DRINKS ◼

Heiße Schokolade [heissuh shoh-koh-lah-duh]   hot chocolate
Kaffee (mit Sahne/Milch) [kafay (mit zahnuh/milsh)]   coffee (with cream/milk)
koffeinfreier Kaffee [kof-ay-een-frei-er kafay]   decaffeinated coffee
Tee (mit Milch/Zitrone)   tea (with milk/lemon)
   [tay (mit milsh/tsee-troh-nuh)]

◼ EISDIELE/EISCAFÉ [eiss-deeluh/eiss-kafay] | ICE CREAM PARLOUR ◼

Eis [eiss]   ice cream
  Vanille [van-il-uh]   vanilla
  Schokolade [shoh-koh-lah-duh]   chocolate
  Erdbeer [airt-bair]   strawberry
  Karamel [karamel]   caramel
Eisbecher [eiss-besher]   ice cream sundae
Eiskaffee [eiss-kafay]   iced coffee
Früchtebecher [fruukhte-besher]   fruit and ice cream sundae
Joghurteis [yoh-gurt-eiss]   frozen yoghurt
Schlagsahne/Schlagrahm/   whipped cream
  (Austria:) Schlagobers [shlahk-zah-nuh/
  shlahk-rahm/shlahk-oh-berss]

Spaghettieis [spa-get-ee-eiss]   ice cream pushed through a press and
   served with strawberry sauce, whipped
   cream and shredded coconut to look
   like spaghetti
Zitronensorbet [tsee-troh-nuh zor-bay]   lemon sorbet

LOCAL KNOWLEDGE

Insider Tip

▶ White Gold

Every year from late April to June, everyone in Germany and Switzerland goes absolutely crazy for the latest crop of *Spargel* [shpargel], a large, white, soft variety of asparagus. During the *Spargelsaison* [shpargel-ze-soñ] ("asparagus season"), people can't seem to get enough of the stuff – restaurants advertise it on big blackboards outside, huts selling nothing else spring up on the side of the road, and people throw a *Spargelparty* [shpargel-partee] or six to enjoy a slice of white gold before the season ends. The remarkably quick-growing vegetable is served fresh with boiled potatoes and accompanied with lashings of buttery hollandaise sauce. If you're offered some, jump at the chance – it's not to be missed.

> SUCCESSFUL SHOPPING

Whether you're after chic shoes, the perfect souvenir, a toothbrush or some wholemeal bread, we've equipped you for every eventuality. We've also provided some very handy 'point & show' pictures.

■ AT THE SHOPS | IM GESCHÄFT [im ge-sheft]

Thanks. I'm just looking around.	Danke, ich sehe mich nur um. [dankuh, ish zayuh mish noor um]
Where can I find...?	Wo finde ich ...? [voh finduh ish]
I'd like...	Ich möchte ... [ish mersh-tuh]
Have you got...?	Haben Sie ...? [hahben zee]
Do you take credit cards?	Nehmen Sie Kreditkarten? [naymen zee kray-deet-kartne]
How much is it?	Wie viel kostet es? [vee feel kosstet ess]
That's expensive!	Das ist aber teuer! [dass isst ahber toyer]

SHOPPING

Is there any chance of a discount?	Können Sie am Preis noch etwas machen? [kernen zee am preiss nokh et-vass makhen]
The maximum I'm prepared to pay is...	Ich zahle höchstens … [ish tsah-luh hersh-stenss]
I'll take it/them.	Ich nehme es. [ish naymuh ess]
Can you recommend a... shop?	Können Sie mir ein … -geschäft empfehlen? [kernen zee meer ein … ge-sheft emp-faylen]

OPENING HOURS ÖFFNUNGSZEITEN [erfnungss-tsei-ten]

| open, closed (for holidays/vacation) | offen [o-fen], (wegen Betriebsferien) geschlossen [vaygen betreepss-fairee-en ge-shlossen] |

■SHOPS | GESCHÄFTE [ge-sheftuh]

die Auskunft
[dee owss-kunft]

das Postamt
[dass posst-amt]

die Apotheke
[dee apoh-taykuh]

die Drogerie
[dee droh-ger-ee]

die Bäckerei
[dee bek-er-ei]

der Obst- und Gemüsehändler
[dair oh-psst unt ge-muuze-hendler]

die Metzgerei
[dee mets-gerei]

der Bioladen
[dair bee-oh-lahden]

das Schuhgeschäft
[dass shoo-gesheft]

der Optiker
[dair op-teeker]

der Juwelier
[dair yoo-vay-leer]

das Lederwarengeschäft
[dass lay-der-varen-gesheft]

die Elektrohandlung
[dert aylek-troh-handlung]

das Computerfachgeschäft
[dass komp-yoo-ter-fakh-ge-sheft]

die Fotoartikel m
[dee foh-toh-arteekel]

das Handygeschäft
[dass hendee-ge-sheft]

der Zeitungshändler
[dair tseitungss-hendler]

die Buchhandlung
[dee bookh-handlung]

der Plattenladen
[dair plat-en-lahden]

das Spielwarengeschäft
[dass shpeel-vahren-ge-sheft]

die Weinhandlung
[dee vein-handlung]

das Spirituosengeschäft
[dass shpee-ree-too-oh-zen-ge-sheft]

der Tabakladen
[dair tabak-lahden]

die Sportartikel m
[dee shport-arteekel]

das Blumengeschäft
[dass bloomen-ge-sheft]

der Friseur
[dair freez-uhr]

Haushaltswaren f
[howss-halts-vahren]

das Reisebüro
[dass reize-buuroh]

department store	das Kaufhaus [dass kowf-howss]
flea market	der Flohmarkt [dair floh-markt]
market	der Markt [dair markt]
patisserie (shop selling cakes and pastries)	die Konditorei [dee kondee-to-rei]
shopping centre/mall	das Einkaufszentrum [dass ein-kowfss-tsen-trum]
souvenir shop	der Souvenirladen [dair soo-ven-eer-lahden]

■ THE PHARMACY | APOTHEKE [apoh-taykuh] ■

> At the Doctor's: page 107

Where's the nearest pharmacy?	Wo ist die nächste Apotheke? [voh isst dee naykss-tuh apoh-taykuh]
Can you give me something for...	Geben Sie mir bitte etwas gegen … [gayben zee meer bituh et-vass gaygen]
You need a prescription for this.	Dieses Mittel ist rezeptpflichtig. [dee-zess mitel isst ray-tsept-pflish-tish]
internally/externally	innerlich [in-er-lish]/äußerlich [oyss-er-lish]
on an empty stomach	auf nüchternen Magen [owf nuush-ter-nen mah-gen]
before/after meals	vor/nach dem Essen [for/nahkh daym essen]
let it dissolve in your mouth	im Mund zergehen lassen [im munt tsair-gayen lassen]
antibiotics	das Antibiotikum [dass antee-bee-oh-teekum]
antidote	das Gegengift [dass gaygen-gift]
aspirin	Aspirin nt [asspee-reen]
burn ointment	die Brandsalbe [dee brant-zalbuh]
camomile tea	der Kamillentee [dair ka-mi-len-tay]
circulatory stimulant	das Kreislaufmittel [dass kreiss-lowf-mitel]
condom	das Kondom [dass kon-dohm]
contraceptive pill, morning-after pill	die Antibabypille [dee antee-baybee-pil-uh], die Pille danach [dee pil-uh danahkh]
cough mixture	der Hustensaft [dair hoossten-zaft]
disinfectant	das Desinfektionsmittel [dass dess-infek-tsee-ohnss-mitel]

> Further information: page 56

LOCAL KNOWLEDGE

Insider Tips

> ### Tell me on a Sunday...

Although the laws are gradually changing, the German-speaking world generally closes for business on Sundays. It can seem like the centres of towns have completely shut down for the day in many areas, and you won't find a thing to buy anywhere. Make sure you get your food shopping earlier in the week if you don't want to starve. If you really get stuck, you can often find some shops selling some basic groceries at the nearest *Hauptbahnhof* [howpt-bahn-hohf] ("main railway station"). Don't feel bad – it's not uncommon to spot some other beleaguered tourists with exactly the same problem while you're there.

THE CHEMIST'S/DRUGSTORE | DROGERIE [droh-ger-ee]

die Seife
[dee zeif-uh]

das Deo(~dorant)
[dass dayoh(~doh-rant)]

die Creme
[dee kraym]

das Toilettenpapier
[dass twa-let-en-papeer]

die Zahnbürste
[dee tsahn-buurss-tuh]

die Zahnpasta
[dee tsahn-pass-tah]

die Zahnseide
[dee tsahn-zeid-uh]

Papiertaschentücher nt
[papeer-tashen-tuusher]

das Haarwaschmittel
[dass har-vash-mit-el]

Haarspray nt
[har-shpray]

der Kamm/die Haarbürste
[dair kam/dee har-buurss-tuh]

der Spiegel
[dair shpeegel]

die Nagelfeile
[dee nah-gel-feil-uh]

die Pinzette
[dee pin-tset-uh]

die Nagelschere
[dee nah-gel-shair-uh]

das Parfüm
[dass par-fuum]

Tampons m
[tam-ponss]

Damenbinden f
[dahmen-binden]

die Wimperntusche
[dee vimpern-too-shuh]

der Lippenstift
[dair lip-en-shtift]

die Rasierklinge
[dee raz-eer-klinguh]

der Rasierapparat
[dair razeer-apa-raht]

das Rasierwasser
[dass razeer-vasser]

das Kondom
[dass kond-ohm]

die Sonnencreme
[dee zon-en-kraym]

die Wärmflasche
[dee vairm-flash-uh]

das Pflaster
[dass pflasster]

Ohropax nt
[ohr-oh-pakss]

die Nadel
[dee nahdel]

der Faden
[dair fahden]

die Sicherheitsnadel
[dee zisher-heits-nahdel]

der Knopf
[dair knopf]

ELECTRICAL GOODS/COMPUTING/PHOTOGRAPHY
ELEKTRO/COMPUTER/FOTO [aylek-troh/komp-yooter/fohtoh]

die Taschenlampe
[dee tashen-lampuh]

die Glühbirne
[dee gluu-birnuh]

die Batterie
[dee bateree]

der Adapter
[dair adapter]

der Laptop
[dair leptop]

das Ladekabel (Laptop)
[dass lahde-kahbel (leptop)]

die CD/die DVD
[dee tsay-day/dee day-fow-day]

der Memorystick
[dair may-moh-ree-stik]

der Drucker
[dair druk-er]

der Scanner
[dair sken-er]

das Handy
[dass hendee]

das Ladekabel (Handy)
[dass lahde-kahbel (hendee)]

der Fernseher
[dair fairn-zayr]

das Radio
[dass rah-dee-oh]

der MP3-Player/der iPod
[dair em-pay-drei-playr/dair ei-pod]

der Kopfhörer
[dair kopf-her-rer]

die Digitalkamera
[dee dee-gee-tahl-kam-er-ah]

das Teleobjektiv
[dass taylay-op-yek-teef]

der Akku
[dair ak-oo]

die Speicherkarte
[dee shpeish-er-kartuh]

der Film
[dair film]

das Dia
[dass dee-a]

die Unterwasserkamera
[dee unter-vasser-kamerah]

die Filmkamera
[dee film-kamerah]

der Wecker
[dair vek-er]

der Elektrorasierer
[dair aylek-troh-razeer-er]

die elektrische Zahnbürste
[dee aylek-trishuh tsahn-buurss-tuh]

der Föhn
[dair fern]

drops	Tropfen m [trop-fen]
ear drops	Ohrentropfen m [ohren-trop-fen]
eye drops	Augentropfen m [owgen-trop-fen]
gauze	die Mullbinde [dee mul-binduh]
headache tablets	die Kopfschmerztablette [dee kopf-shmairts-tablet-uh]
insect repellent	das Insektenmittel [dass in-zekten-mitel]
insulin	Insulin nt [in-zoo-leen]
(tincture of) iodine	das (die) Jod(~tinktur) [dass (dee) yoht(~tinktoor)]
laxative	das Abführmittel [dass ap-fuur-mit-el]
medicine	das Medikament [dass may-dee-ka-ment]
mouthwash	das Mundwasser [dass munt-vasser]
ointment	die Salbe [dee zalbuh]
painkillers	Schmerztabletten f [shmairts-tablet-en]
powder	das Puder [dass pooder]
prescription	das Rezept [dass ray-tsept]
remedy	das Mittel [dass mit-el]
sedative, tranquilizer	das Beruhigungsmittel [dass beroo-igungss-mit-el]
side effects	Nebenwirkungen f [nayben-virkungen]
sleeping tablets	Schlaftabletten f [shlahf-tablet-en]
sticking plasters/ adhesive bandages	das Pflaster [dass pflasster]
stomach pain relief	Magentropfen m [mahgen-trop-fen]
sunburn	der Sonnenbrand [dair zon-en-brant]
suppositories	das Zäpfchen [dass tsepf-shen]
thermometer	das Fieberthermometer [dass feeber-tairmoh-mayter]
throat lozenges	Halstabletten f [halss-tableten]

LOCAL
KNOWLEDGE

Insider Tip

> ### Just what the Doctor ordered...

The sale of medication is much more closely regulated in the German-speaking world than you'll be used to on your native shores. You'll find it much harder to get your hands on even relatively simple painkillers that can be bought in the supermarket back home. Don't worry – you'll still get everything you need, it'll just cost more and you'll have to know where to look. Contrary to what you might think, you won't have much luck in a *Drogerie* [droh-ger-ee], a shop that sells lots of toiletries but very few drugs (if any at all). To pick up your medications, head to a specialist *Apotheke* [apoh-taykuh] ("pharmacy") instead. You'll often have to talk to the (highly trained) pharmacists first before you can get what you want.

SHOPPING

■ THE HAIRDRESSER'S | FRISEUR [freezuhr]

Can I make an appointment for tomorrow?	Kann ich für morgen einen Termin vereinbaren? [kan ish fuur morgen einen tair-meen fair-ein-bah-ren]
Wash and cut/dry cut, please.	Schneiden mit/ohne Waschen, bitte. [shneiden mit/ohnuh vashen, bituh]
A bit shorter./Not too short./Very short, please.	Etwas kürzer./Nicht zu kurz./Ganz kurz, bitte. [et-vass kuur-tser/nisht tsoo kurts/gants kurts, bituh]
Would you trim my moustache/beard, please.	Stutzen Sie mir bitte den Bart. [shtut-sen zee meer bituh dayn bart]
Thank you. That's fine.	Vielen Dank. So ist es gut. [feelen dank zoh isst ess goot]

beard, moustache	der Bart [dair bart], der Schnurrbart [dair shnoor-bart]
blow dry v	föhnen [fernen]
colour/dye v (permanent)	färben [fair-ben]
colour/dye v (semi-permanent)	tönen [tern-en]
comb v	kämmen [kem-en]
curls	Locken f [lok-en]
cut the ends	Spitzen f schneiden [shpitsen shneiden]
dandruff	Schuppen f [shup-en]
do someone's hair	frisieren [free-zeeren]
fringe	der Pony [dair ponee]
hair	das Haar [dass har]
haircut, hairstyle	der Haarschnitt [dair har-shnit], die Frisur [dee free-zoor]
highlights	die Strähne [dee shtray-nuh]
layers	Stufen f [shtoofen]
parting	der Scheitel [dair shei-tel]
pluck (your) eyebrows	Augenbrauen f zupfen [owgen-browen tsup-fen]
straighten	glätten [glet-en]

■ CLOTHING | KLEIDUNG [kleidung]

Can you show me...?	Können Sie mir … zeigen? [kernen zee meer … tsei-gen]
Can I try it on?	Kann ich es anprobieren? [kan ish ess an-proh-beeren]
What size do you take?	Welche Größe haben Sie? [velshuh grer-suh hahben zee]
It's too small/big.	Das ist mir zu klein/groß. [dass isst meer tsoo klein/grohss]
It's a good fit. I'll take it.	Das passt gut. Ich nehme es. [dass passt goot ish naymuh ess]
It's not quite what I wanted.	Das ist nicht ganz, was ich möchte. [dass isst nisht gants, vass ish mershtuh]
Do you have it in a different colour?	Haben Sie das auch noch in einer anderen Farbe? [hahben zee dass owkh nokh in einer anderen farbuh]
Thank you, I'll have to think about it.	Danke, ich denke nochmals darüber nach. [dankuh, ish denkuh nokh-mahlss da-ruuber nahkh]

das T-Shirt
[dass tee-shirt]

der Pullover
[dair pul-ohver]

der Kapuzenpullover
[dair kapoot-sen-pul-ohver]

die Jacke
[dee yak-uh]

die Hose
[dee hoh-zuh]

Shorts f
[shorts]

der Rock
[dair rok]

der Gürtel
[dair guur-tel]

die Bluse
[dee bloo-zuh]

das Hemd
[dass hemt]

das Sakko
[dass zak-oh]

die Strickjacke
[dee shtrik-yakuh]

der Anzug
[dair an-tsook]

das Kleid
[dass kleit]

das Kostüm
[dass koss-tuum]

der Mantel
[dair mantel]

die Strumpfhose
[dee shtrumpf-hohzuh]

Unterwäsche f
[unter-veshuh]

der Bademantel
[dair bahde-mantel]

Socken m/**Strümpfe** m
[zok-en/shtruumpf-uh]

die Badehose
[dee bahde-hohzuh]

der Badeanzug
[dair bahduh-an-tsook]

der Bikini
[dair bee-kee-nee]

die Mütze
[dee muu-tsuh]

der Hut
[dair hoot]

die Handschuhe
[dee hant-shoo-uh]

der Schal
[dair shahl]

▮FOOD & DRINK | LEBENSMITTEL [laybenss-mit-el] ▮

> You'll find an extensive list of culinary delights in the FOOD & DRINK chapter starting on page 36.

What's that?	Was ist das? [vass isst dass]
Can I try it?	Kann ich es probieren? [kan ish ess proh-beeren]
Do you sell...	Verkaufen Sie ...? [fair-kowfen zee]
organic products?	Bioprodukte [bee-oh-proh-duk-tuh]
local products?	Produkte aus der Region [proh-duktuh owss dair ray-gee-ohn]
I'd like...	Geben Sie mir bitte ... [gayben zee meer bituh]
a kilo of...	ein Kilo ... [ein keeloh]
a piece of...	ein Stück von ... [ein shtuuk fon]
a packet of...	eine Packung ... [einuh pakung]
a tin of..., a bottle of...	eine Dose ... [einuh dohzuh], eine Flasche ... [einuh flashuh]
a bag, please.	eine Einkaufstüte. [einuh ein-kowfss-tuu-tuh]
Thanks, that's everything.	Danke, das ist alles. [dankuh, dass isst al-ess]

beer	das Bier [dass beer]
beverages/drinks	Getränke nt [ge-trenkuh] > page 45, 52, 53
bread	das Brot [dass broht] > page 43
butter	die Butter [dee but-er] > page 43, 46
cake	der Kuchen [dair kookhen]
cheese	der Käse [dair kayzuh] > page 43, 50
chicken	das Hähnchen [dass hayn-shen]
chocolate	die Schokolade [dee shoh-koh-lah-duh]
chocolate bar	der Schokoriegel [dair shoh-koh-reegel]
coffee	der Kaffee [dair kafay] > page 46, 53
cold cuts	der Aufschnitt [dair owf-shnit]
cookies/biscuits	Kekse m [kayk-zuh]
cream	die Sahne [dee zahn-uh]
dairy products	Milchprodukte [milsh-proh-duk-tuh] > page 43

LOCAL KNOWLEDGE

Insider Tip

Whatever the Weather

Come rain, wind or snow – keep your chin up and remember a wonderful German saying: *Es gibt kein schlechtes Wetter, es gibt nur falsche Kleidung.* – There's no such thing as bad weather, just inadequate clothing.

eggs	Eier nt [ei-er] > page 43, 46
fish	Fisch m [fish]
flour	das Mehl [dass mayl]
fresh	frisch [frish]
fruit	das Obst [dass oh-psst] > page 42
garlic	der Knoblauch [dair knoh-blowkh]
ice cream	das Eis (die Eiscreme) [dass eiss (dee eiss-kraym)] > page 53
jam	die Marmelade [dee marmuh-lah-duh] > page 46
margarine	die Margarine [dee mar-ga-reenuh]
mayonnaise	die Mayonnaise [dee mayon-ayzuh]
meat	das Fleisch [dass fleish] > page 44, 47, 48
milk	die Milch [dee milsh] > page 43
mineral water	das Mineralwasser [dass mee-ner-ahl-vasser]
mustard	der Senf [dair zenf]
non-alcoholic beer	das alkoholfreie Bier [dass alkoh-hohl-frei-uh beer]
noodles	Nudeln f [noodeln]
nuts	Nüsse (sing die Nuss) [nuuss-uh (dee nuss)]
oil	das Öl [dass erl]
orange juice	der Orangensaft [dair ohrañ-zjen-zaft]
organic food	die Biokost [dee bee-oh-kosst]
patisserie (cakes and pastries)	Backwaren [bak-varen] > page 43, 46
pepper	der Pfeffer [dair pfef-er]
poultry	das Geflügel [dass ge-fluugel]
(without) preservatives	(ohne) Konservierungsstoffe m [(ohnuh) konzair-veerungss-shtof-uh]
preserves/tinned food	Konserven f [konzairven]
salad	der Salat [dair zalaht]
salt	das Salz [dass zalts]
sausage	das Würstchen [dass vuursst-shen]
sausage	die Wurst [dee vursst]
skimmed milk	die fettarme Milch [dee fet-armuh milsh]
soda/pop	die Limonade [dee leemoh-nahduh]
soup	die Suppe [dee zup-uh]
spices	Gewürze nt [ge-vuurts-uh]
(without) sugar	(ohne) Zucker m [(ohnuh) tsuk-er]
sweets	Süßigkeiten f [zuuss-ish-kei-ten]
tea	der Tee [dair tay]
tea bag	der Teebeutel [dair tay-boy-tel]
toast	der Toast [dair tohsst]
vegetables	das Gemüse [dass ge-muu-zuh] > page 41, 49, 50
vinegar	der Essig [dair essish]
wholemeal	Vollkorn nt [fol-korn]
wine	der Wein [dair vein]
yoghurt	Joghurt m/nt [yoh-gurt]

SHOPPING

■ THE OPTICIAN'S | OPTIKER [opteeker]

Could you repair these glasses for me, please?	Würden Sie mir bitte diese Brille reparieren? [vuurden zee meer bituh deezuh bril-uh ray-pa-ree-ren]
I'm short-sighted/long-sighted.	Ich bin kurz-/weitsichtig. [ish bin kurts-/veit-zish-tish]
What's your prescription...?	Wie ist Ihre Sehstärke …? [vee isst eeruh zay-shtair-kuh]
in the right eye,	rechts/im rechten Auge [reshts/im reshten owge],
in the left eye	links/im linken Auge [linkss/im linken owge]
I need some...	Ich brauche … [ish browkhuh]
soaking solution	Aufbewahrungslösung f [owf-bevahrungss-lerzung]
cleansing solution	Reinigungslösung f [reinigungss-lerzung]
for hard/soft contact lenses.	für harte/weiche Kontaktlinsen. [fuur hartuh/veishuh kontakt-linzen]
I'm looking for...	Ich suche … [ish zookhuh]
daily disposable lenses.	Eintageslinsen f. [ein-tah-gess-lin-zen]
some sunglasses.	eine Sonnenbrille. [einuh zon-en-briluh]
some binoculars.	ein Fernglas. [ein fairn-glahss]

■ THE JEWELLER'S | SCHMUCKWAREN [shmuk-varen]

My watch doesn't work.	Meine Uhr geht nicht mehr. [meinuh oor gayt nisht mair]
Could you have a look at it?	Können Sie mal nachsehen? [kernen zee mahl nahkh-zayen]
I'd like a nice souvenir/present.	Ich möchte ein schönes Andenken/Geschenk. [ish mershtuh ein sherness an-denken/ge-shenk]

bracelet	das Armband [dass armbant]
brooch	die Brosche [dee brosh-uh]
costume jewellery	der Modeschmuck [dair moh-de-shmuk]
crystal	der Kristall [dair kriss-tal]
earrings	die Ohrringe m [dee or-ring-uh]
genuine	echt [esht]
gold	Gold nt [golt]
jewellery	Schmuck m [shmuk]
necklace	die Kette [dee ket-uh]
pearl	die Perle [dee pairl-uh]
pendant	der Anhänger [dair an-henger]
ring	der Ring [dair ring]
silver	Silber nt [zilber]
(precious) stone	der (Edel~)Stein [dair (ay-del~)shtein]
waterproof	wasserdicht [vasser-disht]
wristwatch	die Armbanduhr [dee armbant oor]

■THE SHOE SHOP | SCHUHGESCHÄFT [shoo-ge-sheft]

I'd like a pair of... shoes	Ich hätte gern ein Paar … -schuhe.
	[ish het-uh gairn ein par … shoo-uh]
I take a size...	Ich habe Schuhgröße … [ish hahbuh shoo-grer-suh]
They're too narrow/wide.	Sie sind zu eng/weit. [zee zint tsoo eng/veit]
boots	die Stiefel [dee shteefel]
(with) heels	(mit) Absatz m [(mit) ap-zats]
hiking boots	Wander-/Trekkingschuhe m [dair vander-/trek-ing-shoo-uh]
ladies' shoes	Damenschuhe m [dair dah-men-shoo-uh]
leather/rubber sole	die Leder-/Gummisohle [dee lay-der-/gum-ee-zoh-luh]
men's shoes	Herrenschuhe m [dair hair-en-shoo-uh]
moccasins	Mokassins m [dair moh-kass-een]
sandals	Sandalen f [zan-dah-len]
trainers	Turnschuhe m [turn-shoo-uh]
wellies, gum/rubber boots	die Gummistiefel [dair gumee-shteefel]
shoes	Schuhe m [shoo-uh]
shoe polish	die Schuhcreme [dee shoo-kraym]

■SOUVENIRS | SOUVENIRS [soo-ven-eerss]

I'd like...	Ich hätte gern … [ish het-uh gairn]
a nice souvenir.	ein schönes Andenken. [ein sherness an-denken]
something that's typical of this region.	etwas Typisches aus dieser Gegend.
	[et-vass tuu-pish-ess owss deezer gaygent]
I'd like something that's not too expensive.	Ich möchte etwas Preisgünstiges.
	[ish mershtuh et-vass preiss-guunss-tig-ess]
That's lovely.	Das ist aber hübsch. [dass isst ahber huupsh]
Can you gift wrap it for me, please?	Können Sie mir das bitte als Geschenk verpacken?
	[kernen zee meer dass bituh alss ge-shenk fair-pak-en]
Thanks, but I didn't find anything (I liked).	Danke schön, ich habe nichts gefunden
	(das mir gefällt). [dankuh shern, ish hahbuh nishts ge-funden
	(dass meer ge-felt)]
ceramics	Keramik f [kair-ah-mik]
genuine	echt [esht]

hand-made	handgemacht [hant-ge-makht]
jewellery	Schmuck m [shmuk]
local products, local specialities	regionale Produkte nt [raygee-ohn-ah-luh proh-duk-tuh], regionale Spezialitäten f [raygee-ohn-ah-luh shpay-tsee-alee-tay-ten]
pottery	Töpferwaren f [terp-fer-varen]
souvenir	Mitbringsel nt [mitbring-zel]
textiles	Textilien f [tekss-tee-lee-en]
wood sculptures/carvings	Schnitzereien f [shnit-se-rei-en]

STATIONERY AND BOOKS
SCHREIBWAREN UND BÜCHER [shreip-vahren unt buusher]

I'd like...	Ich hätte gern … [ish het-uh gairn]
an English newspaper.	eine englische Zeitung. [einuh en-glish-uh tseit-ung]
a magazine.	eine Zeitschrift. [einuh tseit-shrift]
a travel guide.	einen Reiseführer. [einen reize-fuurer]
a novel in English.	einen englischen Roman. [einen en-glishen roh-mahn]
a detective novel.	einen Kriminalroman. [einen kree-mee-nahl-roh-mahn]
ballpoint pen/biro	der Kugelschreiber [dair koogel-shreiber]
cookbook	das Kochbuch [dass kokh-bookh]
envelope	der Briefumschlag [dair breef-um-shlahk]
eraser	der Radiergummi [dair ra-deer-gum-ee]
glue	der Klebstoff [dair klayp-shtof]
hiking map of the area	die Wanderkarte dieser Gegend [dee vander-kartuh deezer gaygent]
magazine	die Zeitschrift [dee tseit-shrift]
map	die Landkarte [dee lant-kartuh]
newspaper	die Zeitung [dee tseit-ung]
notepad	der Notizblock [dair noh-teets-blok]
novel	der Roman [dair roh-mahn]
paper	das Papier [dass papeer]
paperback	das Taschenbuch [dass tashen-bookh]
pencil	der Bleistift [dair blei-shtift]
playing card	die Spielkarte [dee shpeel-kartuh]
postcard	die Postkarte [dee posst-karte]
road map	die Straßenkarte [dee shtrah-sen-kartuh]
sketchbook	der Zeichenblock [dair tsei-shen-blok]
stamp	die Briefmarke [dee breef-markuh]
town map	der Stadtplan [dair shtat-plahn]
writing/letter paper	das Briefpapier [dass breef-papeer]

>A ROOM WITH A VIEW

Service with a smile: whether you want to pay a bill by credit card, access your hotel's Wi-Fi or get childcare at a holiday resort – all you have to do is ask!

GENERAL INFORMATION

 Planning Your Trip: page 8

Can you recommend..., please?	Können Sie mir bitte ... empfehlen? [kernen zee meer bituh ... emp-faylen]
a hotel, a guesthouse	ein Hotel [ein hoh-tel], eine Pension [einuh penzee-ohn]
a campsite	einen Campingplatz [einen kemping-plats]
Can you recommend anywhere nearby?	Können Sie mir bitte etwas in der Nähe empfehlen? [kernen zee meer bituh et-vass in dair nayuh emp-faylen]

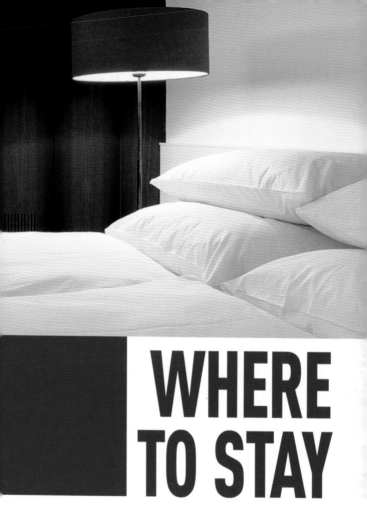

WHERE TO STAY

AT A HOTEL

■RECEPTION DESK | REZEPTION [ray-tsep-tsee-ohn] ■■■■■■

I've reserved a room.	Ich habe ein Zimmer reserviert. [ish hahbuh ein tsim-er rayzair-veert]
My name is...	Mein Name ist … [mein nahmuh isst]
Have you got any vacancies?	Haben Sie noch Zimmer frei? [hahben zee nokh tsim-er frei]
...for one night.	… für eine Nacht. [fuur einuh nakht]
...for two days.	… für zwei Tage. [fuur tsvei tahguh]
...for a week.	… für eine Woche. [fuur einuh vokhuh]

No, I'm afraid we're full.	Nein, wir sind leider vollständig belegt.
	[nein, veer zint leider fol-shtend-ish be-laykt]
No, sorry.	Nein, leider nicht. [nein, leider nisht]
Yes, what sort of room would you like?	Ja, was für ein Zimmer wünschen Sie?
	[yah, vass fuur ein tsim-er vuunshen zee]
a single room	ein Einzelzimmer
	[ein ein-tsel-tsim-er]
a double room	ein Doppelzimmer
	[ein dop-el-tsim-er]
with a shower	mit Dusche
	[mit doosh-uh]
with a bath	mit Bad [mit baht]
a quiet room	ein ruhiges Zimmer
	[ein roo-igess tsim-er]
with a view of the sea	mit Blick aufs Meer [mit blik owfss mair]
Can I see the room?	Kann ich das Zimmer ansehen? [kan ish dass tsim-er an-zayen]
Can you put a third bed in the room?	Können Sie noch ein drittes Bett dazustellen?
	[kernen zee nokh ein drittes bet dah-tsoo-shtel-en]
Do you have Wi-Fi?	Haben Sie WLAN? [hahben zee vay-lahn]
How much is the room with...	Was kostet das Zimmer mit ... [vass kosstet dass tsim-er mit]
breakfast?	Frühstück? [fruu-shtuuk]
breakfast and an evening meal (half board)?	Halbpension? [halp-penzee-ohn]
full board?	Vollpension? [fol-penzee-ohn]
What time is breakfast?	Ab wann gibt es Frühstück? [ap van geept ess fruu-shtuuk]
Where's the restaurant?	Wo ist das Restaurant? [voh isst dass ress-toh-rañ]
Please wake me at... o'clock in the morning.	Wecken Sie mich bitte morgen früh um ... Uhr.
	[vek-en zee mish bituh morgen fruu um ... oor]
Can I have my key, please?	Meinen Schlüssel, bitte. [meinen shluussel bituh]

> Breakfast: FOOD & DRINK, page 46

■COMPLAINTS | BEANSTANDUNGEN [buh-an-shtand-un-gen]

The room hasn't been cleaned.	Das Zimmer ist nicht geputzt worden.
	[dass tsim-er isst nisht ge-putst vorden]
The shower...	Die Dusche ... [dee dooshuh]
The toilet flush...	Die Spülung ... [dee shpuu-lung]
The heating...	Die Heizung ... [dee hei-tsung]
The light...	Das Licht ... [dass lisht]
...doesn't work.	... funktioniert nicht. [funk-tsee-oh-neert nisht]

There's no (warm) water.	Es kommt kein (warmes) Wasser.
	[ess komt kein (varmess) vasser]
The toilet/washbasin is blocked.	Die Toilette/Das Waschbecken ist verstopft.
	[dee twa-let-uh/dass vash-bek-en isst fair-shtopft]

DEPARTURE | ABREISE [ap-reizuh]

What time do I have to check out by?	Wann muss ich spätestens auschecken?
	[van muss ish shpay-tess-tenss owss-cheken]
Can I leave my luggage/ baggage here until (this evening), please?	Kann ich mein Gepäck bis (heute Abend) hierlassen?
	[kan ish mein ge-pek biss (hoytuh ahbent) heer-lassen]
I'm leaving this evening/ tomorrow at... o'clock.	Ich reise heute Abend/morgen um … Uhr ab.
	[ish reizuh hoytuh ahbent/morgen um … oor ap]
Can I have the bill/ check, please.	Machen Sie bitte die Rechnung fertig.
	[makhen zee bituh dee resh-nung fair-tish]
Can I pay by credit card?	Nehmen Sie Kreditkarten? [naymen zee kray-deet-karten]
Thank you very much for everything. Goodbye!	Vielen Dank für alles. Auf Wiedersehen!
	[feelen dank fuur aless owf-vee-der-zayen]

adapter	der Adapter [dair adapter]
air conditioning	die Klimaanlage [dee kleemah-an-lah-guh]
baby monitor	das Babyfon [dass bay-bee-fohn]
babysitting service	die Kinderbetreuung [dee kinder-be-troy-ung]
bathrobe/dressing gown	der Bademantel [dair bah-de-man-tel]
bathroom	das Badezimmer [dass bah-de-tsim-er]
bed	das Bett [dass bet]

LOCAL KNOWLEDGE

Insider Tip

No more night-time arguments...

Every night when they crawl between the sheets, couples all over Germany do something that might seem rather revolutionary to readers from the English-speaking world. Instead of sharing a double eiderdown, each partner in a German relationship often has a single duvet to call their very own. No more fighting for the covers in the night? No more waking up freezing cold at 2am with your partner hogging the sheets? Why didn't we think of this before?!

bed and breakfast	die Übernachtung mit Frühstück [dee uuber-nakh-tung mit fruu-shtuuk]
bed linen	die Bettwäsche [dee bet-veshuh]
bedside table	der Nachttisch [dair nakh-tish]
breakfast	das Frühstück [dass fruu-shtuuk]
breakfast room	der Frühstücksraum [dair fruu-shtuukss-rowm]
(chamber)maid	das Zimmermädchen [dass tsim-er-mayt-shen]
clean v	reinigen [rei-ni-gen]
cot	das Kinderbett [dass kind-air-bet]
cupboard	der Schrank [dair shrank]
dinner (evening meal)	das Abendessen [dass ahbent-essen]
dry cleaner's	die (Sofort~)Reinigung [dee (zohfort~)rein-igung]
floor (storey)	die Etage [dee ay-tah-zjuh]
full board	die Vollpension [dee fol-penzee-ohn]
half board	die Halbpension [dee halp-penzee-ohn]
heating	die Heizung [dee hei-tsung]
high season	die Hauptsaison [dee howpt-ze-zoñ]
iron n	das Bügeleisen [dass buugel-eizen]
key	der Schlüssel [dair shluuss-el]
lamp	die Lampe [dee lampuh]
low season	die Nebensaison [dee nay-ben-ze-zoñ]
lunch	das Mittagessen [dass mit-ahk-essen]
pillow	das Kopfkissen [dass kopf-kissen]
playroom	das (Kinder~)Spielzimmer [dass (kinder~)shpeel-tsim-er]
plug	der Stecker [dair shtek-er]
porter	der Portier [dair por-tee-ay]
reading lamp	die Nachttischlampe [dee nakh-tish-lampuh]
reception	die Rezeption [dee ray-tsep-tsee-ohn]
reservation	die Reservierung [dee ray-zair-veer-ung]
restaurant	das Restaurant [dass ress-toh-rañ]
room	das Zimmer [dass tsim-er]
safe	der Safe [dair sayf]
shower	die Dusche [dee dooshuh]
socket (electric)	die Steckdose [dee shtek-dohzuh]
tap/faucet	der Wasserhahn [dair vasser-hahn]
toilet	die Toilette [dee twa-let-uh]
toilet paper	das Toilettenpapier [dass twa-let-en-pa-peer]
towel	das Handtuch [dass han-tookh]
washbasin	das Waschbecken [dass vash-bek-en]
(cold/hot) water	(kaltes/warmes) Wasser nt [(kaltess/varmess) vasser]
Wi-Fi	WLAN [vay-lahn]
window	das Fenster [dass fen-ster]

IN A HOLIDAY HOME

 Planning Your Trip: page 7

Is electricity/water included in the price?	Ist der Strom-/Wasserverbrauch im Mietpreis enthalten? [isst dair shtrohm-/vasser-fair-browkh im meet-preiss ent-halten]
Are bed linen and towels provided?	Sind Bettwäsche und Handtücher vorhanden? [zint bet-veshuh unt hant-tuusher for-handen]
Are pets allowed?	Sind Haustiere erlaubt? [zint howss-tee-ruh air-lowpt]
Where can I pick up the keys?	Wo kann ich die Schlüssel abholen? [voh kan ish dee shluussel ap-hohlen]
Do we have to clean the apartment before we leave?	Müssen wir die Endreinigung selbst übernehmen? [muussen veer dee ent-rei-ni-gung zelpsst uuber-naymen]

additional costs	Nebenkosten [nayben-kossten]
bed linen	die Bettwäsche [dee bet-veshuh]
bedroom	das Schlafzimmer [dass shlahf-tsim-er]
bottle opener	der Flaschenöffner [dair flashen-erfner]
corkscrew	der Korkenzieher [dair korken-tseer]
day of arrival	der Anreisetag [dair anrei-ze-tahk]
deposit (down payment)	die Anzahlung [dee an-tsah-lung]
deposit (security)	die Kaution [dee kow-tsee-ohn]
electricity	der Strom [dair shtrohm]
end-of-stay cleaning	die Endreinigung [dee ent-rei-ni-gung]
flat/apartment	das Appartement [dass apar-te-mañ]
holiday camp	die Ferienanlage [dee fairee-en-an-lah-guh]
holiday flat/apartment	die Ferienwohnung [dee fairee-en-voh-nung]
holiday home	das Ferienhaus [dass fairee-en-howss]
key	der Schlüssel [dair shluussel]
kitchenette	die Kochnische [dee kokh-nee-shuh]
landlord/lady	der Hausbesitzer m [dair howss-be-zits-er], die Hausbesitzerin f [dee howss-be-zits-er-in]
pets	Haustiere nt [howss-teeruh]
rent n	die Miete [dee meetuh]
rubbish/garbage	der Müll [dair muul]
sofa bed	die Schlafcouch [dee shlahf-kowtsh]
rent v	vermieten [fair-meeten]
towel, dishcloth	das Handtuch [dass hant-tookh], das Geschirrtuch [dass ge-shir-tookh]
waste sorting/separation	die Mülltrennung [dee muul-tren-ung]

der Teller
[dair tel-er]

Gläser (sing das Glas)
[glayzer (dass glahss)]

die Tasse
[dee tassuh]

der Eierbecher
[dair ei-er-besher]

die Gabel
[dee gah-bel]

der Löffel
[dair lerfel]

das Messer
[dass messer]

der Kaffeelöffel
[dair kafay-lerfel]

der Rührlöffel
[dair ruur-lerfel]

der Pfannenwender
[dair pfan-en-vender]

die Schöpfkelle
[dee sherpf-keluh]

der Schneebesen
[dair shnay-bay-zen]

die Reibe
[dee rei-buh]

das Schneidebrett
[dass shnei-de-bret]

das Küchensieb
[dass kuushen-zeep]

der Mixer
[dair mikss-er]

der Topf
[dair topf]

die Pfanne
[dee pfan-uh]

die Schüssel
[dee shuuss-el]

der Gasherd
[dair gahs-hairt]

der Herd/der Backofen
[dair hairt/dair bak-oh-fen]

der Kühlschrank
[dair kuul-shrank]

die Geschirrspülmaschine
[dee ge-shir-shpuul-ma-shee-nuh]

die Waschmaschine
[dee vash-ma-shee-nuh]

der Wasserkocher
[dair vasser-kokher]

die Kaffeemaschine
[dee kafay-ma-shee-nuh]

der Kaffeefilter
[dair kafay-filter]

der Toaster
[dair tohss-ter]

der Staubsauger
[dair shtowp-zowger]

der Wischmopp
[dair vish-mop]

der Bügeleisen
[dass buugel-eizen]

die Wäscheleine
[dee vesh-uh-lein-uh]

der Besen
[dair bayzen]

die Kehrschaufel
[dee kair-show-fel]

das Putzmittel
[dass puts-mit-el]

der Eimer
[dair ei-mer]

AT A CAMPSITE

Have you got room for another caravan/tent?	Haben Sie noch Platz für einen Wohnwagen/ein Zelt? [hahben zee nokh plats fuur einen vohn-vahgen/ein tselt]
How much does it cost per day and per person?	Wie hoch ist die Gebühr pro Tag und Person? [vee hoh-kh isst dee ge-buur proh tahk unt pair-zohn]
What's the price for...	Wie hoch ist die Gebühr für … [vee hoh-kh isst dee ge-buur fuur]
a car?	ein Auto? [ein owtoh]
a caravan (Am: a trailer)?	einen Wohnwagen? [einen vohn-vahgen]
a mobile home?	ein Wohnmobil? [ein vohn-mohbeel]
a tent?	ein Zelt? [ein tselt]
We'll be staying for... days/weeks.	Wir bleiben … Tage/Wochen. [veer bleiben … tahguh/vokhen]
Is there a grocery store here?	Gibt es hier ein Lebensmittelgeschäft? [geept ess heer ein laybenss-mit-el-ge-sheft]
Where are...	Wo sind … [voh zint]
the toilets?	die Toiletten? [dee twa-let-en]
the washrooms?	die Waschräume? [dee vash-roy-muh]
the showers?	die Duschen? [dee dooshen]
Are there any electric hook-up points here?	Gibt es hier Stromanschluss? [geept ess heer shtrohm-an-shluss]
Where can I exchange gas bottles?	Wo kann ich Gasflaschen umtauschen? [voh kan ish gahss-flashen um-towshen]

LOCAL KNOWLEDGE

Inside Tips

The Youth of Today...

The Youth Hostel is a German invention. The very first one was set up in the town of Altena in 1909 by one Richard Schirrmann, a teacher who felt compelled to do something about the lack of inexpensive places for young people to stay in his native country. Part of the castle that Schirrmann used for his original project has been turned into a museum today, but it's still taking bookings if you want to spend the night. And if Schirrmann's ideal whets your appetite for more, the German-speaking world is full of fantastic hotels for you to discover. Whether you want to stay in a floating hostel in Berlin, sleep in a converted vintage car in Dresden, or spend the night in an award-winning concrete masterpiece in Basel, you really will be spoilt for choice.

WHERE TO STAY

barbeque/grill	der Grill [dair gril]
bottle opener	der Flaschenöffner [dair flashen-erfner]
campsite	der Campingplatz [dair kemping-plats]
candles	Kerzen f [kair-tsen]
charcoal	die Grillkohle [dee gril-kohluh]
cooker	der Kocher [dair kokher]
corkscrew	der Korkenzieher [dair korken-tseer]
cutlery	das Essbesteck [dass ess-be-shtek]
drinking water	das Trinkwasser [dass trink-vasser]
electric hook-up point	der Stromanschluss [dair shtrohm-an-shluss]
gas bottle	die Gasflasche [dee gahss-flash-uh]
gas cooker	der Gaskocher [dair gahss-kokher]
hammer, spade	der Hammer [dair ham-er], der Spaten [dair shpah-ten]
hire	leihen [lei-en]
hire charge	die Leihgebühr [dee lei-ge-buur]
methylated spirits	der Brennspiritus [dair bren-shpee-ree-tuss]
paraffin, paraffin lamp	das Petroleum [dass pay-troh-lay-um], die Petroleumlampe [dee pay-troh-lay-um-lam-puh]
pocket knife	das Taschenmesser [dass tashen-messer]
sink	das Geschirrspülbecken [dass ge-shir-shpuul-bek-en]
sleeping bag	der Schlafsack [dair shlahf-zak]
socket (electric)	die Steckdose [dee shtek-dohzuh]
tent peg	der Hering [dair hairing]
tin/can opener	der Dosenöffner [dair dohzen-erfner]
torch/flashlight	die Taschenlampe [dee tashen-lampuh]
water	das Wasser [dass vasser]

AT A YOUTH HOSTEL

Can I hire…?	Kann ich bei Ihnen … leihen? [kan ish bei eenen … lei-en]
…bedding	… Bettwäsche f [bet-veshuh]
…a sleeping bag	… einen Schlafsack [einen shlahf-zak]
The front door is locked at midnight.	Die Eingangstür wird um 24 Uhr abgeschlossen. [dee ein-gangss-tuur virt um feer-unt-tsvan-tsish oor ap-ge-shloss-en]

dormitory	der Schlafsaal [dair shlahf-zahl]
kitchen	die Küche [dee kuushuh]
membership card	die Mitgliedskarte [dee mit-gleets-kartuh]
washroom	der Waschraum [dair vash-rowm]
Wi-Fi	WLAN nt [vay-lahn]
youth hostel	die Jugendherberge [dee yoo-gent-hair-bair-guh]

> WHAT DO YOU WANT TO DO?

Whether you want an authentic cooking course, an exciting
hiking trip or a great evening of theatre: the next few pages will
help you experience loads of holiday adventures.

GENERAL INFORMATION

I'd like a town/city map of..., please.	Ich möchte einen Stadtplan von ... haben. [ish mersh-tuh einen shtat-plahn fon ... hahben]
What tourist attractions are there here?	Welche Sehenswürdigkeiten gibt es hier? [velshuh zay-enss-vuur-dish-kei-ten geept ess heer]
Are there bus tours of the city?	Gibt es Stadtrundfahrten? [geept ess shtat-runt-farten]
How much does the tour cost?	Was kostet die Rundfahrt? [vass koss-tet dee runt-fart]

A PACKED SCHEDULE

SIGHTSEEING/MUSEUMS

When is the museum open?
: Wann ist das Museum geöffnet?
[van isst dass moo-zay-um guh-erfnet]

When does the tour start?
: Wann beginnt die Führung?
[van begint dee fuurung]

Is there a guided tour in English?
: Gibt es auch eine Führung auf Englisch?
[geept ess owkh einuh fuurung owf en-glish]

Is this/that…?
: Ist das …? [isst dass]

altar	der Altar [dair altar]
architecture	die Architektur [dee ar-shee-tek-toor]
audio guide	der Audioguide [dair owdee-oh-geit]
building	das Gebäude [dass ge-boy-duh]
castle	die Burg [dee burk], das Schloss [dass shloss]
cathedral	die Kathedrale [dee ka-tay-drah-luh], der Dom [dair dohm]
cemetery	der Friedhof [dair freet-hohf]
century	das Jahrhundert [dass yar-hun-dert]
chapel	die Kapelle [dee ka-pel-uh]
church	die Kirche [dee kir-shuh]
day trip	der Tagesausflug [dair tahgess-owss-flook]
emperor, empress	der Kaiser [dair keizer], die Kaiserin [dee keizer-in]
excavations	Ausgrabungen f [owss-grah-bun-gen]
exhibition	die Ausstellung [dee owss-shtel-ung]
fortress	die Festung [dee fess-tung]
gallery	die Galerie [dee gal-er-ee]
guide	der Fremdenführer [dair fremden-fuurer]
guided tour	die Führung [dee fuurung]
king, queen	der König [dair kernish], die Königin [dee kernig-in]
monument	das Denkmal [dass denk-mahl]
museum	das Museum [dass moo-zay-um]
painter	der Maler [dair mahler], die Malerin [dee mahler-in]
painting	das Gemälde [dass ge-mayl-duh]
palace	das Schloss [dass shloss], der Palast [dair palasst]
picture	das Bild [dass bilt]
pilgrimage site	der Wallfahrtsort [dair val-farts-ort]
religion	die Religion [dee ray-lee-gee-ohn]
restore (refurbish)	restaurieren [ress-tow-ree-ren]
ruin n	die Ruine [dee roo-ee-nuh]
sculptor	der Bildhauer [dair bilt-hower]
sculpture	die Skulptur [die skulp-toor], die Plastik [dee plasstik]
service (relig.)	der Gottesdienst [dair go-tess-deensst]
sights	Sehenswürdigkeiten f [zayenss-vuur-dish-kei-ten]
sightseeing tour of the town/city	die Stadtrundfahrt [dee shtat-runt-fart]
square	der Platz [dair plats]
the old town	die Altstadt [dee alt-shtat]
tour	die Besichtigung [dee be-zish-ti-gung]
tower	der Turm [dair turm]
town hall, city hall	das Rathaus [dass raht-howss]

A PACKED SCHEDULE

TRIPS & TOURS

What time are we meeting?	Wann treffen wir uns? [van tref-en veer unss]
Where are we meeting?	Wo ist der Treffpunkt? [voh isst dair tref-punkt]
Will we go past the...?	Kommen wir am/an … vorbei? [kom-en veer am/an … for-bei]
Are we going to see..., too?	Besichtigen wir auch …? [be-zish-ti-gen veer owkh]
When are we coming back?	Wann fahren wir zurück? [van fahren veer tsoo-ruuk]

amusement park	der Freizeitpark [dair frei-tseit-park]
botanical garden	Botanischer Garten m [dair boh-tah-nish-er garten]
cave	die Höhle [dee her-luh]
countryside	die Landschaft [dee lant-shaft]
covered market	die Markthalle [dee markt-hal-uh]
day trip	der Tagesausflug [dair tah-gess-owss-flook]
fishing port/harbour	der Fischerhafen [dair fisher-hah-fen]
forest	der Wald [dair valt]
game/wildlife park	der Wildpark [dair vilt-park]
inland	das Landesinnere [dass landess-in-er-uh]
island round-trip	die Inselrundfahrt [dee inzel-runt-fart]
lake	der See [dair zay]
market	der Markt [dair markt]

LOCAL KNOWLEDGE

Insider Tips

Mind your Ps and Queues

British readers in particular might feel rubbed up the wrong way when waiting for something in the German-speaking world. You might be used to forming an orderly queue at home, but don't be too polite here or you might get left behind – especially when trying to get on and off public transport. Instead, try to embrace the Germanic concept of *aktives Anstehen* (lit: active waiting), and be a bit more proactive about making your way to the front if you don't want to find yourself left out in the cold.

Don't Dance

Strange but true: in some parts of Germany and Switzerland you'll still find a *Tanzverbot* [tanss-fair-boht] ("dancing ban") in force on some religious holidays (e.g. Good Friday). This means that's actually illegal to strut your stuff in public all day (although you'll be pleased to know you can bust as many moves as you like in the privacy of your own home). Some clubs get round the law by organising "private parties", but it's also not completely unknown to walk into a venue and find everyone sitting down on the – usually heaving – dance floor.

mountain	der Berg [dair bairk]
mountain range	das Gebirge [dass ge-birg-uh]
mountain village	das Bergdorf [dass bairk-dorf]
national park	der Nationalpark [dair natsee-oh-nahl-park]
nature reserve	das Naturschutzgebiet [dass nat-oor-shuts-ge-beet]
peak (mountain)	der Gipfel [dair gipfel]
pilgrimage site	der Wallfahrtsort [dair val-farts-ort]
ravine	die Schlucht [dee shlukht]
river	der Fluss [dair fluss]
sea	das Meer [dass mair]
spring (of water)	die Quelle [dee kvel-uh]
tour (round trip)	die Rundfahrt [dee runt-fart]
trip	der Ausflug [dair owss-flook]
vantage point	der Aussichtspunkt [dair owss-zishts-punkt]
waterfall	der Wasserfall [dair vasser-fal]
zoo	der Zoo [dair tsoh]

AFTER DARK

■ PUB/BAR/CLUB | KNEIPE/BAR/CLUB [kneipuh/bar/klup] ■

What's on...	Was ist ... los? [vass isst ... lohss]
this weekend?	dieses Wochenende [dee-zess vokhen-enduh]
this evening?	heute Abend [hoytuh ahbent]
What is there to do here in the evenings?	Was kann man hier abends unternehmen? [vass kan man heer ahbents unter-naymen]
Is there a nice pub here?	Gibt es hier eine gemütliche Kneipe? [geept ess heer einuh ge-muut-lishuh knei-puh]
Is there a nightclub here?	Gibt es hier einen Club? [geept ess heer einen klup]
Where can we go dancing?	Wo kann man hier tanzen gehen? [voh kan man heer tan-tsen gayen]
What kind of music do they play here?	Welche Musikrichtung wird hier gespielt? [velshuh moo-zeek-rish-tung virt heer ge-shpeelt]
Is there a dress code?	Ist Abendgarderobe erwünscht? [isst ahbent-garduh-rohbuh air-vuunsht]
A (draught/draft) beer, please.	Ein Bier (vom Fass), bitte. [ein beer (fom fass), bituh]
A whisky and soda, please.	Ein Whisky-Soda, bitte. [ein viss-kee-zoh-dah, bituh]
A glass of red wine, please.	Ein Glas Rotwein, bitte. [ein glahss roht-vein, bituh]
The same again, please.	Das Gleiche noch einmal, bitte. [dass gleish-uh nokh ein-mahl, bituh]
This round's on me.	Diese Runde übernehme ich. [deezuh runduh uuber-naymuh ish]
Shall we dance?	Wollen wir tanzen? [vol-en veer tantsen]

A PACKED SCHEDULE

band	die Band [dee bant]
bar, club, disco	die Bar [dee bar], der Club [dair klup], die Diskothek [dee diss-koh-tayk]
bouncer	der Türsteher [dair tuur-shtayr]
dance v	tanzen [tan-tsen]
gay/lesbian scene	die Schwulen-/Lesbenszene [dee shvoolen-/lez-ben-tsay-nuh]
go out	ausgehen [owss-gayen]
live music	die Livemusik [dee leif-moo-zeek]
party	die Party [dee partee]
pub/bar	die Kneipe [dee knei-puh]

THEATRE/CONCERT/CINEMA
THEATER/KONZERT/KINO [tay-ah-ter/kon-tsairt/kee-noh]

Have you got a calendar of events for this week?	Haben Sie einen Veranstaltungskalender für diese Woche? [hahben zee einen fair-an-shtal-tungss-kal-en-der fuur deezuh vokhuh]
What's on at the theatre tonight?	Welches Stück wird heute Abend im Theater gespielt? [velshess shtuuk virt hoytuh ahbent im tay-ah-ter ge-shpeelt]
Can you recommend a good play?	Können Sie mir ein gutes Theaterstück empfehlen? [kern zee meer ein gootess tay-ah-ter-shtuuk emp-faylen]
When does the performance start?	Wann beginnt die Vorstellung? [van begint dee for-shtel-ung]
Where can I get tickets?	Wo bekommt man Karten? [voh bekomt man karten]
(Two) tickets for this evening, please.	Bitte (zwei) Karten für heute Abend. [bituh (tsvei) karten fuur hoytuh ahbent]
A programme/playbill, please.	Kann ich bitte ein Programm haben? [kan ish bituh ein proh-gram hahben]
Where's the cloakroom?	Wo ist die Garderobe? [voh isst dee garduh-roh-buh]

audio guide	der Audioguide [dair ow-dee-oh-geit]
advance booking	der Vorverkauf [dair for-fair-kowf]
ballet	das Ballett [dass ba-let]
box office	die Kasse [dee kassuh]
calendar of events	der Veranstaltungskalender [dair fair-an-shtalt-ungss-kal-en-der]
cinema	das Kino [dass kee-noh]
film/movie	der Film [dair film]
opera	die Oper [dee oh-per]
performance/screening	die Vorstellung [dee for-shtel-ung]
play	das Schauspiel [dass show-shpeel]
premiere	die Premiere [dee pre-mee-air-uh]
theatre	das Theater [dass tay-ah-ter]
ticket	die Eintrittskarte [dee ein-trits-kartuh]

CELEBRATIONS/EVENTS
FESTE/VERANSTALTUNGEN [fesstuh/fair-an-shtalt-ung-en]

Could you tell me when the... festival takes place, please?	Könnten Sie mir bitte sagen, wann das ...-Festival stattfindet? [kernten zee meer bituh zahgen, van dass ... fess-teeval shtat-findet]
from... to.../every (2) years	vom ... bis .../alle (zwei) Jahre [fom ... biss .../aluh (tsvei) yahruh]
every year in August	jedes Jahr im August [yay-dess yar im ow-gusst]
Can anyone take part/join in?	Kann jeder teilnehmen? [kan yay-der teil-nay-men]
carnival	der Karneval [dair karneval]
circus	der Zirkus [dair tsir-kuss]
fair/fête/street party	die Kirmes [dee kir-mess]
festival	das Festival [dass fess-teeval]
fireworks	das Feuerwerk [dass foyer-vairk]
flea market	der Flohmarkt [dair floh-markt]
funfair	der Jahrmarkt [dair yar-markt]
Shrove Tuesday, Mardi Gras	Faschingsdienstag [fashingss-deenss-tahk]
May Day	der Maifeiertag [dair mei-fei-er-tahk]
parade, procession	der Umzug [dair um-tsook], die Prozession [dee proh-tsess-ee-ohn]

AT THE BEACH & SPORTS

AT THE BEACH | AM STRAND [am shtrant]

Is there a strong current?	Ist die Strömung stark? [isst dee shtrer-mung shtark]
Is it dangerous for children?	Ist es für Kinder gefährlich? [isst ess fuur kinder ge-fair-lish]
When is low tide/high tide?	Wann ist Ebbe/Flut? [van isst eb-uh/floot]
beach	der (Bade~)Strand [dair (bahduh~)shtrant]
changing rooms	Umkleidekabinen f [um-klei-duh-kabee-nen]
current	die Strömung [dee shtrer-mung]
jellyfish	die Qualle [dee kva-luh]
kiosk	der Kiosk [dair kee-ossk]
lifeguard	der Bademeister [dair bahde-meisster]
nudist beach	der FKK-Strand [dair eff-kah-kah-shtrant]
sand	der Sand [dair zant]
shower	die Dusche [dee dooshuh]
sunshade/parasol	der Sonnenschirm [dair zon-en-shirm]
swim v	schwimmen [shvim-en]

A PACKED SCHEDULE

ACTIVE HOLIDAYS/SPORT
AKTIVURLAUB/SPORT [akteef-oor-lowp/shport]

What sports facilities are there here?	Welche Sportmöglichkeiten gibt es hier? [velshuh shport-merk-lish-keiten geept ess heer]
Is there a... here?	Gibt es hier ein/eine ...? [geept ess heer ein/einuh]
Where can I hire...?	Wo kann ich ... ausleihen? [voh kan ish ... owss-lei-en]
I'd like to take a... course for beginners/an advanced... course.	Ich möchte einen ...-kurs für Anfänger/Fortgeschrittene machen. [ish mershtuh einen ... kurss fuur an-fenger/fort-ge-shrit-en-uh makhen]

contest/match	der Wettkampf [dair vet-kampf]
defeat	die Niederlage [dee needer-lahguh]
draw/tie n	unentschieden [un ent-sheeden]
lose v	verlieren [fair-lee-ren]
match/game	das Spiel [dass shpeel]
race	das Rennen [dass ren-en]
referee/umpire	der Schiedsrichter [dair sheets-rishter]
team/crew	die Mannschaft [dee man-shaft]
victory/win n	der Sieg [dair zeek]
win v	gewinnen [ge-vin-en]

WATER SPORTS WASSERSPORT [vasser-shport]

boat hire	der Bootsverleih [dair bohts-fair-lei]
boating licence/permit	der Bootsführerschein [dair bohts-fuurer-shein]
canoe	das Kanu [dass kanoo]
houseboat	das Hausboot [dass howss-boht]
indoor pool	das Hallenbad [dass ha-len-baht]
inflatable/rubber dinghy/boat	das Schlauchboot [dass shlowkh-boht]
motorboat	das Motorboot [dass mohtor-boht]
open air pool	das Freibad [dass frei-baht]
pedalo/pedal boat	das Tretboot [dass trayt-boht]
pick-up service	der Rückholservice [dair ruuk-hohl-sair-viss]
rowing boat	das Ruderboot [dass rooder-boht]
sailing	das Segeln/der Segeltörn [dass zaygeln/dair zaygel-tern]
sailing boat	das Segelboot [dass zaygel-boht]
sailing school	die Segelschule [dee zaygel-shooluh]
surf school	die Surfschule [dee serf-shooluh]
surfboard	das Surfbrett [dass serf-bret]
surfing	das Surfen [dass serf-en]
water skiing	das Wasserskilaufen [dass vasser-shee-lowfen]
windsurfing	das Windsurfen [dass vint-zerfen]

DIVING TAUCHEN [towkh-en]
breathing/oxygen apparatus	das Sauerstoffgerät [dass zower-shtof-ge-rayt]
dive v	tauchen [towkh-en]
diving equipment	die Taucherausrüstung [dee towkh-er-owss-ruuss-tung]
diving mask	die Taucherbrille [dee towkh-er-bril-uh]
diving school	die Tauchschule [dee towkh-shooluh]
flippers	Schwimmflossen f [shvim-flossen]
go snorkelling	schnorcheln [shnor-sheln]
harpoon	die Harpune [dee har-poonuh]
scuba diving	das Gerätetauchen [dass ge-ray-tuh-towkh-en]
snorkel	der Schnorchel [dair shnor-shel]
wetsuit	der Neoprenanzug [dair nay-oh-prayn-an-tsook]

FISHING ANGELN [an-geln]
Where can I go fishing?	Wo kann man hier angeln? [voh kan man heer an-geln]
bait	der Köder [dair kerder]
deep-sea fishing	das Hochseefischen [dass hoh-kh-zay-fishen]
fishing licence	der Angelschein [dair an-gel-shein]
fishing rod	die Angel [dee an-gel]
go fishing	angeln [an-geln]
off/close season	die Schonzeit [dee shohn-tseit]

BALL GAMES BALLSPIELE [bal-shpee-luh]
ball	der Ball [dair bal]
basketball	der Basketball [dair bahss-ket-bal]
football	der Fußball [dair fooss-bal]
football ground	der Fußballplatz [dair fooss-bal-plats]
football team	die Fußballmannschaft [dee fooss-bal-man-shaft]
goal	das Tor [dass tor]
goalkeeper	der Torwart [dair tor-vart], die Torfrau [dee tor-frow]
net	das Netz [dass nets]
volleyball	der Volleyball [dair vo-lee-bal]

TENNIS, ETC. TENNIS UND ÄHNLICHES [teniss unt ayn-lish-ess]
badminton	Badminton nt [bat-min-ten]
covered (tennis) court	die Tennishalle [dee tenis-hal-uh]
racket/racquet	der Schläger [dair shlayger]
squash	Squash nt [skvosh]
table tennis	Tischtennis nt [tish-teniss]
tennis	Tennis nt [teniss]
tennis court	der Tennisplatz [dair teniss-plats]
tennis racket/racquet	der Tennisschläger [dair teniss-shlayger]

A PACKED SCHEDULE

FITNESS & WEIGHT TRAINING   FITNESS- UND KRAFTTRAINING [fit-ness unt kraft-tray-ning]

aerobics	Aerobic f/nt [air-oh-bik]
fitness centre	das Fitnesscenter [dass fit-ness-tsenter]
fitness training	das Konditionstraining [dass kondee-tsee-ohnss-tray-ning]
go jogging/jog v	joggen [jog-en]
weight training	das Krafttraining [dass kraft-tray-ning]
yoga, Pilates	Yoga m/nt [yohgah], Pilates nt [pee-lah-tess]

WELLBEING   WELLNESS [vel-ness]

acupressure	die Akupressur [dee akoo-press-oor]
aromatherapy	die Aromatherapie [dee arohmah-taira-pee]
baths/bathhouse	Bäder (sing das Bad) [bay-der (dass baht)]
beauty treatment	die Beautybehandlung [dee byoo-tee-be-hant-lung]
hammam, Turkish bath	der Hamam [dair ham-ahm]
diet foods	die Diätkost [dee dee-ayt-kosst]
manicure	die Maniküre [dee manee-kuuruh]
massage	die Massage [dee massah-zjuh]
pedicure	die Pediküre [dee pay-dee-kuuruh]
skin peeling treatment	das Peeling [dass peeling]
sauna	die Sauna [dee zow-nah]
solarium	das Solarium [dass zoh-lah-ree-um]
steam room	das Dampfbad [dass dampf-baht]

CYCLING   RADFAHREN [raht-fahren]

bicycle/bike	das Fahrrad [dass far-raht]
crash helmet	der Fahrradhelm [dair far-raht-helm]
cycle path	der Fahrradweg [dair far-raht-vayk]
cycle race	das Radrennen [dass raht-ren-en]
cycle tour	die Radtour [dee raht-toor]
cycle v	Rad fahren [raht fahren]
electric bike	das E-Bike [dass ee-beik]
(inner) tube	der Schlauch [dair shlowkh]
mountain bike	das Mountainbike [dass mown-tayn-beik]
pump	die Luftpumpe [dee luft-pumpuh]
(puncture) repair kit	das Flickzeug [dass flik-tsoyk]
racing bike	das Rennrad [dass ren-raht]

HIKING & MOUNTAINEERING   WANDERN UND BERGSTEIGEN [vandern unt bairk-shteigen]

I'd like to go for a hike in the mountains.	Ich möchte eine Bergtour machen. [ish mershtuh einuh bairk-toor makhen]
Can you show me an interesting route on the map?	Können Sie mir eine interessante Route auf der Karte zeigen? [kernen zee meer einuh interessantuh rootuh owf dair kartuh tseigen]

cable car/funicular railway	die Seilbahn [dee zeilbahn]
day trip/excursion	die Tagestour [dee tahgess-toor]
hiking	das Wandern [dass vandern]
hiking map	die Wanderkarte [dee vander-kartuh]
long-distance hiking route	der Fernwanderweg [dair fairn-vander-vayk]
mountaineering	das Bergsteigen [dass bairk-shteigen]
mountain guide	der Bergführer [dair bairk-fuurer]
path	der Wanderweg [dair vander-vayk]
route	die Route [dee rootuh]
safety rope	das Sicherungsseil [dass zisher-ungss-zeil]

RIDING REITEN [reiten]

equestrian holidays	Reiterferien [reiter-fairee-en]
equestrianism/equestrian sports	der Reitsport [dair reit-shport]
horse	das Pferd [dass pfairt]
ride n	reiten [reiten]
riding school	die Reitschule [dee reit-shooluh]
ride v/go riding	der Ausritt [dair owss-rit]

GOLF GOLF [golf]

a round of golf	eine Runde Golf [einuh runduh golf]
eighteen-hole course	der Achtzehn-Loch-Platz [dair akht-tsayn-lokh-plats]
golf club	der Golfschläger [dair golf-shlayger]
golf course	der Parcours [dair parkoor]
green fee	Greenfee nt/f [dass green-fee]
tee	der Abschlag [dair ap-shlahk]
visitor	der Tagesbesucher [dair tah-gess-be-zookher]

IN THE AIR IN DER LUFT [in dair luft]

gliding	das Segelfliegen [dass zaygel-fleegen]
hang gliding	das Drachenfliegen [dass drakhen-fleegen]
parachuting	das Fallschirmspringen [dass fal-shirm-shpringen]
paragliding	das Paragliding [dass para-glei-ding]
parasailing	das Fallschirmsegeln (mit Schleppschirm am Strand) [dass fal-shirm-zaygeln (mit shlep-shirm am shtrant)]

WINTER HOLIDAYS WINTERURLAUB [vintair-oor-lowp]

A day ticket, please.	Eine Tageskarte, bitte. [einuh tah-gess-kartuh, bituh]
What time is the last trip up the mountain/down into the valley?	Um wie viel Uhr ist die letzte Bergfahrt/Talfahrt? [um vee feel oor isst dee let-stuh bairk-fart/tahl-fart]

A PACKED SCHEDULE

binding	die (Ski~)Bindung [dee (shee~)bin-dung]
bottom ski lift station	die Talstation [dee tahl-shtat-see-ohn]
cable car	die Gondel [dee gondel]
cross-country ski course	die Loipe [dee loypuh]
cross-country skiing	Langlauf m [lang-lowf]
day pass	der Tagespass [dair tah-gess-pahss]
(ice) hockey	Eishockey nt [eis-hok-ay]
ice rink	die Eisbahn [dee eiss-bahn]
ice skates	Schlittschuhe m [shlit-shoo-uh]
ice skating	Eislauf m [eiss-lowf]
ski n	der Ski [dair shee]
ski goggles	die Skibrille [dee shee-bril-uh]
ski instructor	der Skilehrer [dair shee-lairer], die Skilehrerin [dee shee-lairer-in]
ski poles	Skistöcke m [shee-shter-kuh]
skiing lessons	der Skikurs [dair shee-kurss]
ski v/go skiing	das Skilaufen [dass shee-lowfen]
snowboard n	das Snowboard [dass snoh-bort]
toboggan	der Schlitten [dair shlit-en]
top ski lift station	die Bergstation [dee bairk-shtat-see-ohn]
week pass	der Wochenpass [dair vokhen-pass]

COURSES

I would like to take a German language course...	Ich interessiere mich für einen Deutsch-Sprachkurs … [ish inter-ess-eeruh mish fuur … einen doytsh-shprahkh-kurss]
for beginners.	für Anfänger. [fuur an-fenger]
for advanced learners.	für Fortgeschrittene. [fuur fort-ge-shri-ten-uh]
Is prior knowledge required?	Sind Vorkenntnisse erforderlich? [zint for-kent-niss-uh air-ford-er-lish]
Are materials included in the price?	Sind die Materialkosten inklusive? [zint dee ma-tair-ee-ahl-kossten in-kloo-zee-vuh]
What should I bring along?	Was ist mitzubringen? [vass isst mit-soo-bringen]

carpentry workshop	die Holzwerkstatt [dee holts-vairk-shtat]
cooking	das Kochen [dass kokhen]
course	der Kurs [dair kurss]
drumming	das Trommeln [dass tromeln]
goldsmithery	das Goldschmieden [dass golt-shmeeden]
life drawing	das Aktzeichnen [dass akt-tseish-nen]
oil painting	die Ölmalerei [dee erl-mahl-er-ei]
photography	das Fotografieren [dass foh-toh-graf-eeren]
watercolour painting	das Aquarellmalen [dass ak-varel-mahlen]

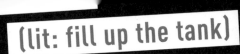

(lit: fill up the tank)

ordentlich tanken [or-dent-lish tanken]

> WORDS GONE WILD

When your dictionary fails you and everyone seems to be talking gobbledegook, you've most likely been plunged headfirst into the wonderful world of slang.

BECOME **AN INSIDER**

Who hasn't been in this situation: you've made some contacts in a foreign land and are excitedly listening to your new friends chatting away – but their speech is littered with mysterious words that quite simply leave you in the dark. That's because there's a world of difference between the language you'll find in the dictionary and the language people actually use on the street. But don't panic: over the next few pages, we'll plunge you headfirst into the lingo that's spoken in cafés, clubs, bars, shops, hotels and hostels, and show you the way people talk when they're chatting on the bus, on the train, and in the lively

WARNING!
SLANG

squares of villages, towns and cities. We've tracked down all the most
authentic, essential and downright funniest slang expressions to give you
some all-important insider knowledge. But beware: there are some phrases
that are better left unsaid! Also, bear in mind that slang is often a very local
affair and that pronunciation can vary from region to region. But with a bit
of patience, you'll be able to get a handle on all the different regional dialects
and listen in on what everyone has to say.
Have fun reading this chapter and broadening your vocabulary!

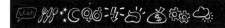

DAY TO DAY

GREETINGS, ETC.

Hallo Leute! [haloh loytuh]	Hi guys/everyone!
Hallo Schatz!/Schätzchen! [haloh shats/shetss-yen]	Hi darling! (lit: treasure)
Moin Digga! [moyn dig-ah]	Hey dude! (in the north of Germany)
Was geht ab?/Was läuft? [vass gayt ap/vass loyft]	What's up?/What's going on?
Na? [na]	Hey, what's up?
Alles klar? [al-ess klar]	How's things?
Wenn man vom Teufel spricht!	Speak of the devil!
[ven man fom toy-fel shprisht]	
Ich muss los. [ish muss lohss]	I gotta dash./I gotta go.
Bis später!/dann! [biss shpayter/dan]	See you later!
Bis gleich!/bald! [biss gleish/balt]	See you soon!
Hallöchen!/Tschüssi! [hal-er-shen/tshuu-see]	Hi!/Bye! (cutesy)

RESPONSES

ja [yah], **nein/nee/nö** [nein/nay/ner]	yes, no
Klar! [klar], **Gerne!** [gair-nuh],	Sure!, I'd love to!
Genau! [ge-now], **Stimmt!** [shtimt]	Exactly!, True that!
Kein Problem/Thema/Ding.	No problem! (lit: problem/theme/thing)
[kein prohb-laym/tay-mah/ding]	
Macht nichts. [makht nishts]	It doesn't matter./Don't worry about it.
Keine Ahnung. [keinuh ah-nung]	I don't have a clue.

COMMANDS

Hör mal ... [her mahl]	Listen…/Listen up…
Pass auf. [pass owf]	Listen up!/Look out!
Warte mal./kurz. [vartuh mahl/kurts]	Wait a second!/Hang on!
Ruhig Blut! [roo-ish bloot]	Keep your hair on! (lit: calm blood)
Reg dich nicht auf. [rayk dish nisht owf]	Stay cool.
Komm mal wieder runter! [kom mahl veeder runter]	Calm down! (lit: come back down again)
Mach dir keinen Kopf! [makh deer keinen kopf]	Don't stress out!/
	Don't worry about it!
Setzt deinen Arsch in Bewegung!	Shift your arse/Move your ass!
[zetst deinen arsh in be-vay-gung]	
Ein bisschen flink! [ein biss-shen flink]	Get a move on!
Mach zu!/Beeil dich! [makh tsoo/buh-eil dish]	Hurry up!

WARNING! SLANG

AMONG FRIENDS...

jdm simsen [yay-man-dem zim-zen]	to send s.o. an SMS/a text message
quatschen [kvat-shen]**/tratschen** [trat-shen]	to chat/to gossip
Schwachsinn erzählen/Quatsch reden	to talk bullshit
[shvakh-zin air-tsay-len/kvatsh ray-den]	
rumhängen/abhängen/herumhängen	to hang out
[rum-hen-gen/ap-hen-gen/hair-um-hen-gen]	
herumblödeln/herumalbern	to monkey around, to goof around
[hair-um-bler-deln/hair-um-al-bern]	
sich totlachen/kranklachen	to laugh yourself to death/laugh
[zish toht-lakh-en/krank-lakh-en]	yourself sick
ins Fettnäpfchen treten	to put your foot in it/in your mouth.
[inss fet-nepf-shen tray-ten]	(lit: to step in the fat trap)
Er/sie nervt mich total an!	He/she really annoys me!
[air/zee nairft mish toh-tahl an]	
Das geht mir auf den Sack.	That gets on my nerves.
[dass gayt meer owf dayn zak]	(lit: on my sack/scrotum)
lügen, dass sich die Balken biegen	to lie through one's teeth
[luugen, dass zish dee balken beegen]	(lit: to lie that the beams are bending)
Er/sie nimmt kein Blatt vor den Mund.	He/she calls a spade a spade.
[air/zee nimt kein blat for dayn munt]	(lit: he/she doesn't put a leaf in front of
	his/her mouth)
sich zum Narren/Affen machen	to make a fool of yourself
[zish tsum na-ren/af-en makhen]	

THAT'S GREAT...

Geil!/Saugeil!/Megageil! [geil/zow-geil/may-gah-geil]	Amazing! (lit: horny)
Supergeil! [zooper-geil]	Brilliant! (lit: super horny)
Der Hammer! [dair ham-er]	Amazing! (lit: the hammer!)
Bombastisch! [bom-bass-tish]	Great!
Ich bin super drauf! [ish bin zooper drowf]	I feel great/amazing.
Es geht mir blendend. [ess gayt meer blen-dent]	I feel wonderful.
Alles im grünen Bereich!	Everything's OK!
[aless im gruu-nen be-reish]	(lit: everything's in the green area)
Ich bin auf Wolke sieben! [ish bin owf volkuh zeeben]	I'm on cloud nine! (lit: cloud seven)
Ich fühle mich, als könnte ich Bäume ausreißen.	I feel ready for anything.
[ish fuuluh mish alss kern-tuh ish boy-muh owss-rei-sen]	(lit: I feel I could rip up trees)
von etwas schwärmen [fon et-vass shvair-men]	to rave about sth (lit: to swarm about sth)
ganz aus dem Häuschen sein	to be thrilled to bits (lit: to be completely
[gants owss daym hoyss-shen zein]	out of the little house)
Wahnsinn! [vahn-zin]	Crazy good!

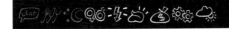

THAT'S BORING...

stinknormal [shtink-nor-mahl]   bog-standard
stinklangweilig [shtink-lang-veil-ish]   mind-numbingly boring
sich zu Tode langweilen [zish tsoo tohduh lang-veilen]   to be bored to death

THAT'S ANNOYING

Du gehst mir auf die Nerven/den Keks.   You get on my nerves.
  [doo gayst meer owf dee nair-fen/dayn kaykss]   (Keks = lit: biscuit/cookie)
jdm auf den Geist/Senkel gehen [yay-man-dem owf   to get on s.o.'s nerves
  dayn geisst/zenkel gayen]   (lit: ghost/shoelaces)
völliger Bockmist [fer-lig-er bok-misst]   complete bullshit
Erzähl mir keine Märchen!   Don't lie to me!
  [air-tsayl meer keinuh mayr-shen]   (lit: don't tell me fairy stories)
Sei nicht sauer auf mich! [zei nisht zow-er owf mish]   Don't be mad (lit: sour) at me!
Das ist grottenschlecht! [dass isst grot-en-shlesht]   That sucks!

FEELING BAD?

Ich bin nicht ganz auf dem Damm!   I'm feeling under the weather.
  [ish bin nisht gants owf daym dam]   (lit: I'm not completely on the dam)
Ich bin fix und fertig/alle. [ish bin fikss unt fair-tish/aluh] I'm completely knackered/tuckered.
eine Stinklaune haben [einuh shtink-low-nuh hahben]   to be in a terrible (lit: stinking) mood
an die Decke/in die Luft gehen   to flip out/hit the ceiling (in anger)
  [an dee dekuh/in dee luft gayen]
am Boden zerstört sein   to be bummed out
  [am bohden tsair-shtert zein]   (lit: to be destroyed on the floor)
ins Bodenlose fallen   to hit rock bottom
  [inss boh-den-loh-zuh fal-en]   (lit: to fall into the bottomless)
Das war eine kalte Dusche für ihn/sie.   That brought him/her down to the
  [dass var einuh kaltuh dooshuh fuur een/zee]   earth with a bump.
                                                               (lit: it was a cold shower for him/her)
ein Pechvogel [ein pesh-foh-gel]   an unlucky devil (lit: an unluck-bird)
Er/sie scheint das Pech abonniert zu haben.   He's/she's always unlucky. (lit: he/she
  [air-zee sheint dass pesh ab-boh-neert tsoo hahben]   seems to have subscribed to bad luck)
eine Nullnummer [einuh nul-num-er]   a loser
Ihm/ihr geht die Muffe. [eem/eer gayt dee muf-uh]   He's/she's shit scared.
Bammel haben [bam-el hahben]   to be scared stiff/to have the jitters
Mir ist mau. [meer isst mow]   I feel sick.
Es ist zum Kotzen! [ess isst tsum kot-sen]   It makes you want to puke!
Mir ist hundeelend. [meer isst hunduh-aylent]   I feel as sick as a dog.

WARNING! SLANG

FOOD

Mir knurrt der Magen. [meer knurt dair mahgen]
My tummy's rumbling.

Ich habe einen Bärenhunger./Ich bin hungrig wie ein Wolf. [ish hahbuh einen bay-ren-hunger/ ish bin hun-grish vee ein volf]
I'm starving.
(lit: I'm as hungry as a bear/wolf)*

Kohldampf haben [kohl-dampf hahben]
to be starving (lit: to have cabbage steam)

Ich sterbe vor Hunger. [ish shtairbuh for hunger]
I'm dying of hunger.

naschen [nashen]
to snack

fressen [fressen], **mampfen** [mamp-fen]
to stuff your face

etwas verschlingen [et-vass fair-shling-en]
to devour sth

sich den Bauch vollschlagen [zish dayn bowkh fol-shlah-gen]
to stuff yourself

ein Loch im Bauch haben [ein lokh im bowkh hahben]
to be starving
(lit: to have a hole in the stomach)

Zum Fingerablecken! [tsum finger-ap-lek-en]
Finger licking good!

Ich bin pappsatt. [ish bin pap-zat]
I'm stuffed.

Das liegt mir wie ein Stein im Magen. [dass leekt meer vee ein shtein im mahgen]
That's sitting like a stone in my stomach.

GOING OUT

▪ DRINKS ▪

die Gerstenlimonade [dee gairss-ten-lee-moh-nah-duh]
beer (lit: hops lemonade)

ein Kurzer [ein kurtser]
a shot/shooter

ein Radler [ein rahd-ler], **ein Alster** [ein al-ster]
a shandy (beer and lemonade)

der Fusel [dair foozel]
booze/hooch

die Puffbrause [dee puf-brow-zuh]
bubbly (lit: brothel soda)

ein Absacker [ein ap-zak-er]
a nightcap

*

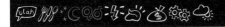

■ AT THE BAR/PUB

eine Kneipe/eine Stammkneipe
[einuh kneipuh/einuh shtam-kneipuh]

eine Kneipentour [einuh knei-pen-toor]

eine Spelunke [einuh shpe-lun-kuh]

eine Bumskneipe/ein Bumslokal
[einuh bumz-knei-puh/ein bumz-loh-kahl]

Lass uns einen trinken gehen.
[lass unss einen trinken gayen]

Lass uns einen heben. [lass unss einen hayben]

Lass uns einen hinter die Binde gießen.
[lass unss einen hinter dee binduh gee-sen]

vorglühen [for-gluu-en]

aufgedonnert/aufgetakelt/aufgemotzt
[owf-ge-don-ert/owf-ge-tah-kelt/owf-ge-motst]

brechend/gerammelt voll [bresh-ent/ge-ra-melt fol]

saufen [zow-fen]

Runter damit! [runter da-mit]

ordentlich tanken [or-dent-lish tanken]

Ex oder Arschloch! [ekss ohder arsh-lokh]

das Tanzbein schwingen [dass tants-bein shving-en]

der Zappelbunker [dair tsap-el-bun-ker]

Geile Mucke! [geiluh muk-uh]

sich die Nacht um die Ohren hauen
[zish dee nakht um dee or-en how-en]

ein Partyparasit [ein par-tee-pa-ra-zeet]

der Türsteher/der Rausschmeißer
[dair tuur-shtay-er/dair rowss-shmeisser]

Hier ist nichts los. [heer isst nishts lohss]

bar/favourite pub

bar crawl

dive bar

drinking hole

Let's go for a drink.

Let's have a drink. (lit: let's lift one up)

Let's get a drink in. (lit: let's throw one behind the collar)

to have pre-drinks (before going out)

tarted up

packed/chock-full

to drink

Down the hatch!

to drink a lot (lit: fill up the tank)

Down/Chug it in one!
(lit: down it or you're an arsehole)

to take to the dance floor
(lit: to swing the dancing leg)

nightclub (lit: a fidget bunker)

Awesome music!

to pull an all-nighter (lit: to hit the night around the ears)

gate crasher (lit: party parasite)

bouncer (lit: door-stander/thrower-outer)

There's nothing going on here./
This place is dead.

WARNING! SLANG

LATER ON...

saufen wie ein Loch [zow-fen vee ein lokh] — to drink heavily (lit: like a hole)
beschickert/angetütert [be-shik-ert/an-getuut-ert] — tipsy
beschwipst/beduselt [be-shvipsst/be-doozelt] — squiffy
stockbetrunken/berauscht/besoffen [shtok-be-trunk-en/be-rowsht/be-zof-en] — drunk

Ich bin blau. [ish bin blow] — I'm completely drunk. (lit: I'm blue)*
saufen bis zum Verlust der Muttersprache [zow-fen biss tsum fair-lusst dair mut-er-shprah-khuh] — to get dead drunk (lit: to drink until you lose the ability to speak your mother tongue)

kotzen [kot-sen], **kübeln** [kuu-beln] — to vomit
eine Pizza legen [einuh pit-sah lay-gen] — to vomit (lit: to lay down a pizza)
göblen [gerb-len] — to vomit from drinking too much
Ich habe einen Kater. [ish hahbuh einen kahter] — I've got a hangover. (lit: I've got a male cat)
ein Katerfrühstück [ein kahter-fruu-shtuuk] — breakfast to cure a hangover

SMOKING

eine Kippe/eine Fluppe/ein Glimmstängel/ eine Rette [einuh kip-uh/einuh flup-uh/ein glim-shten-gel/einuh ret-uh] — cigarette

ein Sargnagel [ein zark-nahgel] — cancer stick (lit: a coffin nail)
Hast du mal 'ne Kippe? [hasst doo mahl ne kip-uh] — Do you have a cigarette?
qualmen wie ein Schlot [kval-men vee ein shlot] — to smoke like a chimney
kiffen [kif-en] — to get high/smoke a joint

MEN & WOMEN

PEOPLE

Typ/Kerl [tuup/kairl] — guy/dude
Tussi/Mädel [tuss-ee/may-del] — chick/girl
eine Zicke [einuh tsik-uh] — a bitch
ein Flittchen [ein flit-shen] — a hussy
Sie hat viel Holz vor der Hütte. [zee hat feel holts for dair huu-tuh] — She's well endowed. (lit: she's got a lot of wood in front of the hut)
ordentlich was in der Hose haben [or-dent-lish vass in dair hohzuh hahben] — to be well hung (lit: to have sth decent in the trousers)
eine Bohnenstange [einuh boh-nen-shtan-guh] — a beanpole

ein Arschkriecher/ein Arschlecker   an arsecrawler/arselicker
[ein arsh-kree-sher/ein arsh-lek-er]
ein Klugscheißer [ein klook-sheisser]   smartarse/smartass
ein Drecksack [ein drek-zak]   dirty bastard
ein Pantoffelheld [ein pan-tof-el-helt]   hen-pecked husband (lit: a slipper-hero)
ein Weiberheld [ein vei-ber-helt]   womaniser (lit: a woman-hero)
ein Schickimicki [ein shik-ee-mik-ee]   fancy-schmancy, trendy type

■ FLIRTING & MORE...

auf jdn stehen [owf yay-man-den shtayen]   to fancy s.o.
jdn angaffen [yay-man-den an-gaf-en]   to ogle s.o.
Ich bin scharf auf ihn/sie. [ish bin sharf owf een/zee]   I've got the hots for him/her.
Er/sie macht mich total an!   He/she really turns me on!
[air/zee makht mish toh-tahl an]
zum Anbeißen gut aussehen   to look good enough to eat (lit: good
[tsum an-bei-sen goot owss-zayen]   enough to bite)
Er/sie hat sich in sie/ihn verknallt.   He's/she's head over heals for her/
[air/zee hat zish in zee/ihn fair-knalt]   him.
flirten [flerten]   to flirt
anbaggern/anquatschen [an-bag-ern/an-kvat-shen]   to chat up
anmachen [an-makh-en]   to chat up/to turn on
jdn abschleppen [yay-man-den ap-shlep-en]   to pick s.o. up
knutschen/rummachen [knoot-shen/rum-makh-en]   to make out
züngeln [tsuun-geln]   to French kiss (lit: to tongue)
die Möpse [dee merp-zuh]   tits
die Eier [dee ei-er]   balls (lit: eggs)
der Po [dair poh]   ass/arse
Geile Kiste! [geil-uh kiss-tuh]   Sensational boobs/arse! (lit: horny box)
eine Latte haben [einuh lat-uh hahben]   to have a hard-on (lit: to have a crossbar)
das Gummi/die Pariser [dass gum-ee/dee paree-zer]   a condom (lit: a rubber/Parisian)
poppen/nageln [pop-en/nah-geln]   to shag/hump (lit: to pop/to nail)
flachlegen [flakh-lay-gen]   to bang (lit: to lay flat)
bumsen/vögeln [bum-zen/fer-geln]   to screw (vögeln = lit: to bird)
ein Quickie [ein kvik-ee]   a quickie
jdn abservieren   ditch/dump s.o.
[yay-man-den ap-zair-veer-en]   (abservieren = lit: clear the table)
Andere Mütter haben auch schöne   There are plenty more fish in the sea.
Töchter/Söhne. [ander-uh muu-ter hahben owkh   (lit: other mothers also have beautiful
sher-nuh tersh-ter/zer-nuh]   daughters/sons)
Aus den Augen, aus dem Sinn.   Out of sight, out of mind.
[owss dayn ow-gen, owss daym zin]
ein Seitensprung [ein zei-ten-shprung]   an affair (lit: a jump to the side)

WARNING! SLANG

RANTING, BITCHING, SWEARING

THE BASICS

Mensch!/Mann! [mensh/man]	Goodness!/Man!
Donnerwetter! [don-er-vet-er]	Gosh! (lit: thunder weather!)
Mist!/Scheiße! [misst/sheissuh]	Shit!
Verdammt noch mal! [fair-damt nokh mahl]	Damn!
Verdammte Scheiße! [fair-dam-tuh sheissuh]	Bloody hell!/Son of a bitch!
Halt's Maul! [halts mowl]	Shut your mouth/gob! (lit: hold your muzzle)
Hau ab! [how ap]	Get lost!
Geh zum Teufel!/Hol dich der Teufel! [gay tsum toy-fel/hohl dish dair toy-fel]	Go screw yourself! (lit: go to the devil!/go fetch the devil!)
Du kannst mich mal! [doo kannst mish mahl]	Bite me!
Arschloch! [arsh-lokh], **Du Arsch!** [doo arsh]	Arse/asshole!, You arse!
jdn verarschen [yay-man-den fair-arsh-en]	to bust s.o.'s balls/take the piss out of s.o.

NUMBSKULLS & NITWITS

Pappnase! [pap-nah-zuh]	Idiot! (lit: cardboard nose)
Trottel! [trot-el]	Jerk!
Tollpatsch! [tol-patsh]	Klutz!/Blunderer!
Spinner! [shpin-er]	Oddball!/Weirdo!
Spinnst du? [shpinsst doo]	Are you crazy? (lit: are you spinning)
dumm wie Stroh [dum vee shtroh]	totally stupid (lit: as dumb as straw)
Er ist nicht ganz dicht. [air isst nisht gants disht]	He's/she's not playing with a full deck.
Er/sie hat keinen blassen Schimmer. [air/zee hat keinen blass-en shim-er]	He/she doesn't have the foggiest idea. (lit: doesn't have a faint glow)
Er/sie hat nicht mehr alle Tassen im Schrank. [air/zee hat nisht mair al-uh tass-en im shrank]	He's/she's a sandwich short of a picnic. (lit: he/she doesn't have all the cups in the cupboard)
Er/sie ist übergeschnappt/durchgedreht. [air/zee isst uuber-ge-shnapt/doorsh-ge-drayt]	He's/she's gone crazy.
Er/sie hat einen Dachschaden. [air/zee hat einen dakh-shah-den]	He's/she's not all there. (he's/she's got roof damage)
Er/sie hat eine Schraube locker. [air/zee hat einuh shrow-buh lok-er]	He/she has a screw loose.

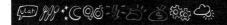

■ MORE INSULTS ■

Was für ein Arschloch! [vass fuur ein arsh-lokh] — What an arse/asshole!
Scheißkerl! [sheiss-kairl] — Prick!/Shitbag!
Weichei!/Warmduscher! [veish-ei/varm-doosh-er] — Wimp! (lit: soft egg/warm-shower-taker)
Rüpel!/Rowdy! [ruupel/row-dee] — Lout!/Thug!
Dussel! [dussel] — Twit!/Dope!
Miststück!/Mistkerl! [misst-shtuuk/misst-kairl] — Douchebag!
Drecksau! [drek-zow] — Filthy swine!
Schlampe!/Biest! [shlam-puh/beesst] — Bitch!
Dumpfbacke! [dumpf-bak-uh] — Dimwit!/Dumbass!
Schwanzkopf! [shvants-kopf] — Dickhead!
Quasselstrippe! [kvassel-shtrip-uh] — Chatterbox!

UNMENTIONABLES

pinkeln/schiffen [pin-keln/shif-en] — to piss
eine Stange Wasser in die Ecke stellen — to take a leak
  [einuh shtang-uh vasser in dee ek-uh shtel-en]   (lit: to place a rod of water in the corner)
kacken/scheißen [kak-en/sheiss-en] — to shit
rülpsen [ruulp-sen] — to burp/belch
ein Bäuerchen machen [ein boy-er-shen makhen] — to burp/belch (lit: to make a little farmer)
furzen/pupsen [furt-sen/poop-zen] — to fart
einen fahren lassen [einen fahren lassen] — to let one go/to fart
Dünnpfiff haben [duun-pfif hahben] — to have diarrhoea/the shits
sich die Seele aus dem Leib kotzen — to vomit
  [zish dee zayluh owss daym leip kot-sen]   (lit: to vomit the soul from your body)

MONEY

■ CASH ■

Knete/Kohle/Moos/Zaster — money/cash/moolah/dough
  [knay-tuh/koh-luh/mohss/tsass-ter]
ein Zwanni [ein tsvan-ee] — a twenty euro note
ein Fuffi [ein fuf-ee] — a fifty euro note
ein Hunni [ein hun-ee] — a hundred euro note
ein Haufen Geld [ein how-fen gelt] — a chunk of change
eine Stange Geld [einuh shtang-uh gelt] — a pile of money

WARNING! SLANG

RICH OR BROKE

Er/sie ist stinkreich. [air/zee isst shtink-reish]
He/she is filthy rich.

ein Schweinegeld verdienen
to be raking it in
[ein shvein-uh-gelt fair-dee-nen]

schweres Geld machen [shvair-ess gelt makhen]
to make a packet (lit: to make heavy money)

sich eine goldene Nase verdienen
to be raking it in
[zish einuh gol-de-nuh nah-zuh fair-dee-nen]
  (lit: to earn a gold nose)

Ich bin pleite/blank. [ish bin plei-tuh/blank]
I'm broke.

knapp bei Kasse sein [knap bei kassuh zein]
to be broke

keinen roten Heller haben
to not have two pennies/
[keinuhn roh-ten hel-er hahben]
  cents to rub together

den Gürtel enger schnallen
to tighten your belt
[dayn guurtel en-ger shnal-en]

sich Geld pumpen [zish gelt pump-en]
to borrow money (lit: to pump)

PRICEY OR PEANUTS

Was kostet der Spaß? [vass kosstet dair shpass]
What's the damage?

Das ist aber happig! [dass isst ahber hap-ish]
That's a bit pricey!

sich dumm und dämlich bezahlen
to pay an arm and a leg
[zish dum unt daym-lish be-tsah-len]
  (lit: to pay yourself dumb and stupid)

spottbillig [shpot-bil-ish]
cheap as chips

für Umme [fuur um-uh]
for free

einen Appel und ein Ei kosten
to cost peanuts
[einen ap-el unt ein ei kossten]
  (lit: an apple and an egg)

Das ist keinen Pfifferling wert.
It's not worth a damn/straw.
[dass isst keinen pfif-er-ling vairt]

SPENDING & EARNING

Geld zum Fenster hinauswerfen
to throw your money out of the
[gelt tsum fensster hin-owss-vair-fen]
  window

Geld verplempern [gelt fair-plem-pern]
to waste money

Geld verjubeln [gelt fair-yoo-beln]
to splurge

jdn abzocken [yay-man-den ap-tsok-en]
to rip s.o. off

jdm Geld aus der Tasche ziehen
to rob s.o. blind
[yay-man-den gelt owss dair tashuh tsee-en]

etwas abstauben/schnorren
to steal sth
[et-vass ap-shtow-ben/shnor-ren]

etwas verscherbeln/verticken
to flog/sell sth
[et-vass fair-shair-beln/vair-tick-en]

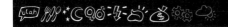

WORK

mit den Hühnern aufstehen
[mit dayn huu-nern owf-shtay-en]

to get up at the crack of dawn
(lit: to get up with the chickens)

schuften [shuf-ten]**, malochen** [malo-khen]

to work hard

sich kaputtarbeiten [zish ka-put-ar-bei-ten]

to slog one's guts out

sich den Arsch abarbeiten [zish dayn arsh ap-ar-bei-ten]

to work your arse/ass off

ein Arbeitssüchtiger/Arbeitsjunkie
[ein arbeits-zuush-tig-er/ar-beitss-jun-kee]

a workaholic

eine ruhige Kugel schieben
[einuh roo-iguh koo-gel shee-ben]

to have a cushy number
(lit: to slide a calm bullet)

Däumchen drehen [doym-shen dray-en]

to twiddle your thumbs

auf der faulen Haut liegen
[owf dair fowlen howt leegen]

to laze around
(lit: to lie on the lazy skin)

ein Faulpelz/ein Bummelant
[ein fowl-pelts/ein bum-el-ant]

slacker/idler/lazybones

sich abseilen [zish ap-zei-len]

to skive/skip work
(lit: to abseil/rappel yourself)

blaumachen/krankfeiern [blow-makhen/krank-fei-ern]

to pull a sickie

etwas in den Sand setzen [et-vass in dayn zant zet-sen]

to screw sth up (lit: to set sth in the sand)

jdm eine Standpauke halten [yay-man-dem einuh
shtant-pow-kuh hal-ten]

to bollock s.o./
to give s.o. a roasting

Ich hab' bei meinem Chef einen Stein im Brett.
[ish hap bei meinem shef einen shtein im bret]

I'm in my boss's good books.
(lit: I've got a stone in my boss's plank)

THE WEATHER

Es regnet Bindfäden.
[ess rayg-net bint-fay-den]

It's raining cats and dogs!
(lit: it's raining threads/cords)

Es schifft! [ess shift]

It's pissing it down!

Es gießt wie aus Kübeln. [ess geesst vee owss kuu-beln]

It's bucketing it down.

klatschnass [klatsh-nass]

soaking wet

wie ein begossener Pudel aussehen
[vee ein be-goss-en-er poodel owss-zayen]

to look like a drowned rat
(lit: a watered poodle)

das Scheißwetter [dass sheiss-vet-er]

shitty weather

Es ist arschkalt da draußen.
[ess isst arsh-kalt dah drow-sen]

It's freezing cold/as cold as hell
outside! (lit: it's arse cold outside)

Es ist tierisch heiß! [ess isst teer-ish heiss]

It's boiling! (lit: it's animal hot)

eine Bullenhitze [einuh bul-en-hit-suh]

scorching heat

ein bisschen Sonne tanken
[ein biss-shen zon-uh tank-en]

to top up your tan
(lit: to put a little sun in the tank)

CREDITS

Cover photograph: Huber-Images: R. Schmid
Photos: Denis Pernath (pp. 2, 3, 6/7, 10/11, 20/21, 54/55, 78/79, 104/105);
Mauritius Images: Alamy (pp. 3, 36/37); Cortina Hotel, Munich (pp. 68/69)
Illustrations: Mascha Greune, Munich
'Point & Show' Pictures/Photos: Lazi&Lazi; Food Collection; Comstock;
stockbyte, Fisch-Informationszentrum e.V.; Fotolia/Christian Jung;
Fotolia/ExQuisine; photos.com
Picture editors: Factor Product, Munich (pp. 2, 3, 6/7, 10/11, 20/21, 36/37,
54/55, 68/69, 78/79, 104/105); red.sign, Stuttgart (pp. 41–45)
'Point & Show' Pictures/Illustrations: Factor Product, Munich; HGV Hanseatische
Gesellschaft für Verlagsservice, Munich (pp. 44/45, 56, 58/59, 63, 66, 73, 75)

1st Edition 2014
Worldwide Distribution: Marco Polo Travel Publishing Ltd, Pinewood, Chineham
Business Park, Crockford Lane, Basingstoke, Hampshire RG24 8AL, United
Kingdom. E-mail: sales@marcopolouk.com
© MAIRDUMONT GmbH & Co. KG, Ostfildern
© based on the PONS English Travel Phrasebook
© PONS GmbH, Stuttgart

Chief editor: Marion Zorn, MAIRDUMONT
Concept and project management: Carolin Schmid, C.C.SCHMID Munich

Edited by: Jacqueline Sword, Hannover
Editing: PONS GmbH, Stuttgart; Kristin Schimpf, MAIRDUMONT, Ostfildern;
Barbara Pflüger, Stuttgart

Local Knowledge, The Menus, Warning! Slang, Dos & Don'ts:
J. Andrews, jonandrews.co.uk

Translated from German by J. Andrews, jonandrews.co.uk
Phonetics by J. Andrews, jonandrews.co.uk
Typesetting & Prepress: M. Feuerstein, Wigel

Coverdesign: Factor Product, Munich
Design content: Zum goldenen Hirschen, Hamburg; red.sign, Stuttgart

Printed in Germany

> READY FOR ANYTHING

At the Doctor's, at the police station or at the bank:
when things get tricky or need to be sorted out fast,
this handy chapter will help you out.

BANK/BUREAU DE CHANGE

 Numbers: Inside front cover

Where's the nearest bank, please?	Wo ist hier bitte eine Bank? [voh isst heer bituh einuh bank]
I'd like to change... pounds (dollars) into euros.	Ich möchte ... Pfund (Dollar) in Euro wechseln. [ish mershtuh ... pfunt (dol-ar) in oy-roh vek-seln]

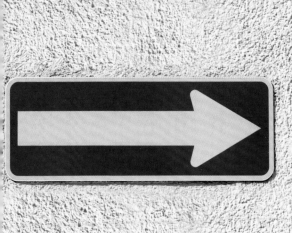

I'd like to change this traveller's cheque/check.	Ich möchte diesen Reisescheck einlösen. [ish mershtuh deezen reize-shek ein-lerzen]
May I see your...	Darf ich bitte … sehen? [darf ish bituh … zayen]
passport, please?	Ihren Pass [eeren pass]
identity card, please?	Ihren Ausweis [eeren owss-veiss]
Sign here, please.	Würden Sie bitte hier unterschreiben? [vuurden zee bituh heer unter-shrei-ben]
The cashpoint won't accept my card.	Der Geldautomat akzeptiert meine Karte nicht. [dair gelt owtoh-maht ak-tsep-teert meinuh kartuh nisht]
The cashpoint has swallowed my card.	Der Geldautomat gibt meine Karte nicht mehr heraus. [dair gelt owtoh-maht geept meinuh kartuh nisht mair hair-owss]

amount	der Betrag [dair betrahk]
bank	die Bank [dee bank]
banknote	der Geldschein [dair gelt-shein]
bureau de change	die Wechselstube [dee vekssel-shtoo-buh]
cash register	die Kasse [dee kassuh]
cashpoint	der Geldautomat [dair gelt-owtoh-maht]
change	das Kleingeld [dass klein-gelt]
change (money) v	wechseln [vek-seln]
cheque/check	der Scheck [dair shek]
coin	die Münze [dee muunt-suh]
counter	der Schalter [dair shalter]
credit card	die Kreditkarte [dee kray-deet-kartuh]
currency	die Währung [dee vay-rung]
euro	der Euro [dair oy-roh]
exchange	der Geldwechsel [dair gelt-vekssel]
exchange rate	der Wechselkurs [dair vekssel-kurss]
form	das Formular [dass formoolar]
money	das Geld [dass gelt]
pay out v	auszahlen [owss-tsahlen]
pin number/code	die Geheimzahl [dee ge-heim-tsahl]
signature	die Unterschrift [dee unter-shrift]
traveller's cheque/check	der Reisescheck [dair reize-shek]

COLOURS

 Point & Show: page 4

black	schwarz [shvarts]
blue	blau [blow]
brown	braun [brown]
colourful	farbig [farbish]
dark blue, dark green	dunkelblau [dunkel-blow], dunkelgrün [dunkel-gruun]
golden	goldfarben [golt-farben]
green	grün [gruun]
grey	grau [grow]
light blue, light green	hellblau [hell-blow], hellgrün [hel-gruun]
orange	orange [ohrañ-zjuh]
pink	rosa [roh-zah]
plain/monochrome	einfarbig [ein-farbish]
purple	lila [leelah]
red	rot [roht]

silver	silberfarben [zilber-farben]
turquoise	türkis [tuur-keess]
violet	violett [vee-oh-let]
white	weiß [veiss]
yellow	gelb [gelp]

AT THE DOCTOR'S

■ INFORMATION | AUSKUNFT [owss-kunft]

Can you recommend a good...?	Können Sie mir einen guten ... empfehlen? [kernen zee meer einen gooten ... emp-faylen]
doctor	Arzt m [artst], Ärztin f [airts-tin]
eye specialist	Augenarzt m [owgen-artst]
gynaecologist	Frauenarzt m [frowen-artst]
ear, nose and throat specialist	Hals-Nasen-Ohren-Arzt m [halss-nahzen-ohren-artst]
dermatologist	Hautarzt m [howt-artst]
pediatrician	Kinderarzt m [kinder-artst]
neurologist	Nervenarzt m [nairfen-artst]
general practitioner	praktischen Arzt m [prak-tishen artst]
urologist	Urologen m [oor-oh-loh-gen]
dentist	Zahnarzt m [tsahn-artst]
Where's his/her surgery/ office?	Wo ist seine/ihre Praxis? [voh isst zeinuh/eeruh prak-siss]

 Pharmacy: page 57, 58, 60

■ AT THE DOCTOR'S | BEIM ARZT [beim artst]

What's the problem?	Was für Beschwerden haben Sie? [vass fuur be-shvairden hahben zee]
It hurts here.	Ich habe hier Schmerzen. [ish hahbuh heer shmairt-sen]
I've hurt myself.	Ich habe mich verletzt. [ish hahbuh mish fair-letst]
I've got a bad cold.	Ich bin stark erkältet. [ish bin shtark air-kel-tet]
I've got a headache.	Ich habe Kopfschmerzen. [ish hahbuh kopf-shmairt-sen]
I've got a sore throat.	Ich habe Halsschmerzen. [ish hahbuh halss-shmairt-sen]
I've got a cough.	Ich habe Husten. [ish hahbuh hooss-ten]
I'm allergic to...	Ich bin allergisch gegen ... [ish bin alairgish gaygen]
antibiotics.	Antibiotika. [an-tee-bee-oh-tee-kah]
bees.	Bienen. [beenen]
pollen.	Pollen. [pol-en]

I'm vaccinated against...	Ich bin gegen … geimpft. [ish bin gaygen … ge-impft]
hepatitis A/B/A and B.	Hepatitis A/B/A und B [hay-pa-tee-tiss ah/bay/ah unt bay]
tetanus.	Tetanus [tay-tan-uss]
typhoid.	Typhus [tuu-fuss]
How often do I have to take it?	Wie oft muss ich es einnehmen? [vee oft muss ish ess ein-nay-men]
I'm prone to allergies.	Ich bin Allergiker. [ish bin alair-gi-ker]
I'm pregnant.	Ich bin schwanger. [ish bin shvanger]
I suffer from...	Ich bin … [ish bin]
diabetes.	Diabetiker. [dee-ab-ay-teeker]
epilepsy.	Epileptiker. [ay-pee-lep-teeker]
Where does it hurt?	Wo tut es weh? [voh toot ess vay]
It's nothing serious.	Es ist nichts Ernstes. [ess isst nishts airnss-tess]
Can you give me/prescribe something for...?	Können Sie mir bitte etwas gegen … geben/verschreiben? [kernen zee meer bituh et-vass gaygen … gayben/fair-shreiben]
I usually take...	Normalerweise nehme ich … [nor-mahler-veizuh naymuh ish]

■ AT THE DENTIST'S | BEIM ZAHNARZT [beim tsahn-artst]

I've got (terrible) toothache.	Ich habe (starke) Zahnschmerzen. [ish hahbuh (shtarkuh) tsahn-shmairt-sen]
This tooth (on the top row/on the bottom row/in the front of my mouth/in the back of my mouth) hurts.	Dieser Zahn (oben/unten/vorn/hinten) tut weh. [deezer tsahn (ohben/unten/forn/hinten) toot vay]
I've lost a filling.	Ich habe eine Füllung verloren. [ish hahbuh einuh fuulung fair-lohren]
I will have to fill the tooth.	Ich muss ihn plombieren. [ish muss een plom-beeren]
I will have to pull out the tooth.	Ich muss ihn ziehen. [ish muss een tsee-en]
I've broken a tooth.	Mir ist ein Zahn abgebrochen. [meer isst ein tsahn ap-ge-brokh-en]
I'd like an injection, please.	Geben Sie mir bitte eine Spritze. [gayben zee meer bituh einuh shprit-suh]
I don't want an injection.	Geben Sie mir bitte keine Spritze. [gayben zee meer bituh keinuh shprit-suh]

■ IN HOSPITAL | IM KRANKENHAUS [im kran-ken howss]

How long will I have to stay here?	Wie lange muss ich hierbleiben? [vee languh muss ish heer bleiben]
When can I get out of bed?	Wann darf ich aufstehen? [van darf ish owf-shtayen]

FROM A TO Z

abdomen	der Unterleib [dair unter-leip]
abscess	der Abszess [dair apss-tsess]
AIDS	Aids nt [ayts]
allergy	die Allergie [dee alair-gee]
anaesthetic	die Narkose [dee nar-koh-zuh]
ankle	der Knöchel [dair kner-shel]
appendix	der Blinddarm [dair blint-darm]
arm	der Arm [dair arm]
artificial limb	die Prothese [dee proh-tay-zuh]
asthma	das Asthma [dass asst-mah]
back	der Rücken [dair ruuken]
backache	Rückenschmerzen m [ruuken-shmairt-sen]
bandage	der Verband [dair fairbant]
belly	der Bauch [dair bowkh]
blackout	die Ohnmacht [dee ohn-makht]
bladder	die Blase [dee blah-zuh]
bleed v	bluten [blooten]
blood	das Blut [dass bloot]
blood poisoning	die Blutvergiftung [dee bloot-fair-giftung]
blood pressure	der Blutdruck [dair bloot-druk]
bone	der Knochen [dair knokhen]
brain	das Gehirn [dass ge-hirn]
brain haemorrhage	der Gehirnschlag [dair ge-hirn-shlahk]
breathe v	atmen [ahtmen]
broken	gebrochen [ge-brokhen]
bronchitis	die Bronchitis [dee bron-shee-tiss]
bruise	die Prellung [dee prel-ung]
bruising	die Quetschung [dee kvet-shung]
burn n	die Verbrennung [dee fair-bren-ung]
bypass	der Bypass [dair bei-pass]
cancer	der Krebs [dair kraypss]
catch a cold	sich erkälten [zish air-kelten]
chest	die Brust [dee brusst]
chickenpox	die Windpocken [vint-pok-en]
chills/shivering	der Schüttelfrost [dair shuutel-frosst]
circulatory disorder	die Kreislaufstörung [dee kreiss-lowf-shter-rung]
cold	der Schnupfen [dair shnupfen]
colic	die Kolik [dee koh-leek]
collarbone	das Schlüsselbein [dass shluussel-bein]
concussion	die Gehirnerschütterung [dee ge-hirn-air-shuut-erung]
constipation	die Verstopfung [dee fair-shtopf-fung]
contagious	ansteckend [an-shtek-ent]
cough	der Husten [dair hooss-ten]
cramp	der Krampf [dair krampf]

cut n	die Schnittwunde [dee shnit-vunduh]
diabetes	der Diabetes [dair dee-ab-ay-tess]
diarrhoea	der Durchfall [dair doorsh-fal]
difficulty breathing	die Atembeschwerden [dee ahtem-be-shvairden]
digestion	die Verdauung [dee fair-dowung]
dizziness	der Schwindel [dair shvindel]
doctor's practice	die Praxis [dee prakssiss]
dress v (a wound)	verbinden [fair-binden]
ear	das Ohr [dass or]
eardrum	das Trommelfell [dass tromel-fel]
examination	die Untersuchung [dee unter-zookhung]
extract (a tooth) v	ziehen [tsee-en]
eye	das Auge [dass ow-guh]
face	das Gesicht [dass ge-zisht]
faint n	die Ohnmacht [dee ohn-makht]
fever	das Fieber [dass feeber]
filling	die Plombe [dee plombuh]
finger	der Finger [dair finger]
flu	die Grippe [dee grip-uh]
food poisoning	die Lebensmittelvergiftung [dee laybenss-mit-el-fair-giftung]
foot	der Fuß [dair fooss]
fracture	der Knochenbruch [dair knokhen-brukh]
fungal infection	die Pilzinfektion [dee pilts-infek-tsee-ohn]
gall bladder	die Gallenblase [dee gal-en-blahzuh]
German measles	Röteln pl [rer-teln]
gullet	die Speiseröhre [dee speizer-er-ruh]
hand	die Hand [dee hant]
head	der Kopf [dair kopf]
headache	Kopfschmerzen m [kopf-shmairt-sen]
heart	das Herz [hairts]
heart attack	der Herzanfall [hairts-an-fal], der Herzinfarkt [hairts-infarkt]
heart defect	der Herzfehler [hairts-fayler]
heart trouble	Herzbeschwerden f [hairts-be-shvairden]
hernia	der Leistenbruch [dair leiss-ten-brukh]
herpes	der Herpes [dair hair-pess]
hip	die Hüfte [dee huuf-tuh]
HIV positive	HIV-positiv [hah-ee-fow-poh-zee-teef]
hospital	das Krankenhaus [dass kranken-howss]
hurt v	wehtun [vay-toon]
ill/sick adj	krank [krank]
illness	die Krankheit [dee krank-heit]
indigestion	die Verdauungsstörung [dee fair-dow-ungss-shter-rung]
infection	die Infektion [dee in-fek-tsee-ohn]

inflammation	die Entzündung [dee ent-tsuun-dung]
inflammation of the middle ear	die Mittelohrentzündung [dee mit-el-or-ent-tsuun-dung]
injection	die Spritze [dee shprit-suh]
injure v	verletzen [fair-let-sen]
injury	die Verletzung [dee fair-let-sung]
insomnia	die Schlaflosigkeit [dee shlahf-loh-zish-keit]
intestines	der Darm [dair darm]
jaundice	die Gelbsucht [dee gelp-zookht]
joint	das Gelenk [dass ge-lenk]
kidney stone	der Nierenstein [dair neeren-shtein]
knee	das Knie [dass knee]
leg	das Bein [dass bein]
lip	die Lippe [dee lip-uh]
liver	die Leber [dee lay-ber]
lower back pain	der Hexenschuss [dair hek-sen-shuss]
lung	die Lunge [dee lunguh]
Lyme disease	die Borreliose [dee bor-ay-lee-oh-zuh]
measles	Masern pl [mah-zern]
medical insurance card	der Krankenschein [dair kranken-shein]
meningitis	die Hirnhautentzündung [dee hirn-howt-ent-tsuun-dung]
menstruation	die Menstruation [dee men-stroo-at-see-ohn]
migraine	die Migräne [dee mee-graynuh]
miscarriage	die Fehlgeburt [dee fayl-geboort]
mouth	der Mund [dair munt]
mumps	Mumps m/f [mumpss]
muscle	der Muskel [dair musskel]
nausea	die Übelkeit [dee uubel-keit]
neck	der Hals [dair halss]
nephritis (kidney inflammation)	die Nierenentzündung [dee neeren-ent-tsuun-dung]
nerve	der Nerv [dair nairf]
nervous	nervös [nairv-erss]
nose	die Nase [dee nahzuh]
nurse	der Krankenpfleger [dair kranken-pflay-ger], die Krankenschwester [dee kranken-shvesster]
operation	die Operation [dee oh-per-at-see-ohn]
pacemaker	der Herzschrittmacher [dair hairt-shrit-makher]
pain	Schmerzen m [shmairt-sen]
paralysis	die Lähmung [dee laymung]
poisoning	die Vergiftung [dee fair-giftung]
polio	die Kinderlähmung [dee kinder-laymung]
pregnancy	die Schwangerschaft [dee shvanger-shaft]
pregnant	schwanger [shvanger]
prescribe	verschreiben [fair-shreiben]

pull/strain (a muscle)	die Zerrung [dee tsairung]
pulse	der Puls [dair pulss]
pus	der Eiter [dair ei-ter]
rash	der Ausschlag [dair owss-shlahk]
reception	der Empfang [dair emp-fang]
rheumatism	das Rheuma [dass roy-mah]
rib	die Rippe [dee rip-uh]
salmonella	Salmonellen pl [zal-moh-nel-en]
scar	die Narbe [dee narbuh]
scarlet fever	der Scharlach [dair shar-lakh]
sciatica	der Ischias [dair ish-ee-ass]
sexual organs	Geschlechtsorgane nt [ge-shlesh-ts-or-gah-nuh]
shin	das Schienbein [dass sheen-bein]
shoulder	die Schulter [dee shulter]
sick/ill adj	krank [krank]
sinusitis	die Stirnhöhlenentzündung [dee shtirn-herlen-ent-tsuun-dung]
skin	die Haut [dee howt]
skull	der Schädel [dair shay-del]
sleeplessness	die Schlaflosigkeit [dee shlahf-loh-zish-keit]
smallpox	Pocken pl [pok-en]
sore throat	Halsschmerzen m [halss-shmairt-sen]
specialist	der Facharzt [dair fakh-artst], die Fachärztin [dee fakh-airts-tin]
sprained	verstaucht [fair-shtow-kht]
sting	der Stich [dair shtish]
stomach	der Magen [dair mahgen]
stomachache	Magenschmerzen m [mahgen-shmairt-sen]
stool (sample)	der Stuhlgang [dair shtool-gang]
stroke	der Schlaganfall [dair shlahk-an-fal]
sunstroke	der Sonnenstich [dair zon-en-shtish]
consultation/office hours	die Sprechstunde [dee shpresh-shtun-duh]
sweat v	schwitzen [shvit-sen]
swelling	die Schwellung [dee shvel-ung]
swollen	geschwollen [gesh-vol-en]
temperature (fever)	das Fieber [dass feeber]
tetanus	der Tetanus [dair tay-tan-uss]
throat	die Kehle [dee kayluh]
tick	die Zecke [dee tsekuh]
toe	die Zehe [dee tsayuh]
tongue	die Zunge [dee tsunguh]
tonsils	Mandeln f [mandeln]
tooth	der Zahn [dair tsahn]
tooth decay	die Karies [dee kah-ree-ess]
torn ligament	der Bänderriss [dair ben-der-riss]
ulcer	das Geschwür [dass ge-shvuur]

ultrasonic scan	die Ultraschalluntersuchung [dee ultrah-shal-unter-zoo-khung]
unconscious	bewusstlos [be-vusst-lohss]
urine	der Urin [dair oo-reen]
vaccination	die Impfung [dee imp-fung]
venereal disease	die Geschlechtskrankheit [dee gesh-leshtss-krank-heit]
virus	das Virus [dass veer-uss]
vomit v	sich erbrechen [zish air-bresh-en]
waiting room	das Wartezimmer [dass var-tuh-tsim-er]
wind n	Blähungen f [blay-un-gen]
wound	die Wunde [dee vunduh]
X-ray v	röntgen [rernt-gen]

INTERNET CAFÉS

Is there an Internet café near here?	Wo gibt es in der Nähe ein Internetcafé? [voh geept ess in dair nayuh ein intairnet-kaf-ay]
What does it cost for an hour/ a quarter of an hour?	Wie viel kostet eine Stunde?/Viertelstunde? [veefeel koss-tet einuh shtunduh/feertel-shtunduh]
Can I skype here?	Kann ich bei Ihnen skypen? [kan ish bei eenen skei-pen]
Can I charge my device here?	Kann ich mein Gerät bei Ihnen aufladen? [kan ish mein ge-rayt bei eenen owf-lahden]
Do you have the right kind of charger for my device?	Haben Sie ein passendes Ladegerät für mich? [hahben zee ein pass-en-dess lah-de-ge-rayt fuur mish]
Can I print out a page?	Kann ich eine Seite ausdrucken? [kan ish einuh zeituh owss-druk-en]
I can't get a connection here.	Hier klappt die Verbindung nicht. [heer klapt dee fair-bindung nisht]
Can I burn some photos from my digital camera onto CD here?	Kann ich bei Ihnen Fotos von meiner Digitalkamera auf CD brennen? [kan ish bei eenen foh-tohss fon meiner dee-gee-tahl-kam-er-ah owf tsay-day bren-en]
Do you have a headset for making phone calls?	Haben Sie auch ein Headset zum Telefonieren? [hahben zee owkh ein het-set tsum tay-lay-foh-neeren]

LOST & FOUND

Where's the lost property office, please?	Wo ist das Fundbüro, bitte? [voh isst dass funt-buuroh, bituh]
I've lost...	Ich habe ... verloren. [ish hahbuh ... fair-lohren]
I left my handbag on the train.	Ich habe meine Handtasche im Zug vergessen. [ish hahbuh meinuh hant-tashuh im tsook fair-gessen]

Please let me know if it's handed in.	Benachrichtigen Sie mich bitte, wenn sie gefunden werden sollte. [be-nahkh-rish-tigen zee mish bituh, ven zee ge-funden vairden zoltuh]
Here's the address of my hotel/my home address.	Hier ist meine Hotelanschrift/Heimatadresse. [heer isst meinuh hoh-tel an-shrift/hei-maht ad-ressuh]

MAIL

Where is...	Wo ist ... [voh isst]
the nearest post office	das nächste Postamt? [dass naykss-tuh posst-amt]
the nearest postbox (mailbox)?	der nächste Briefkasten? [dair naykss-tuh breef-kassten]
How much does it cost to send a letter/postcard...	Was kostet ein Brief/eine Postkarte ... [vass kosstet ein breef/einuh posst-kartuh]
to the UK?/to the US? /to Ireland?/to Canada?	nach Großbritannien/in die USA/nach Irland/ nach Kanada? [nahkh grohss-bree-tan-ee-en/in dee oo-ess-ah/ nahkh eer-lant/nahkh kanadah]
I'd like to send this letter by airmail/express.	Ich möchte diesen Brief per Luftpost/Express schicken. [ish mershtuh deezen breef pair luft-posst/ekss-press shik-en]

address	die Adresse [dee ad-ressuh]
addressee	der Empfänger [dair emp-fenger]
by airmail	per Luftpost f [pair luft-posst]
charge n	die Gebühr [dee ge-buur]
collection	die Leerung [dee lair-ung]
counter	der Schalter [dair shalter]
envelope	der Briefumschlag [dair breef-umshlahk]
express letter	der Eilbrief [dair eil-breef]
fill in	ausfüllen [owss-fuulen]
form	das Formular [dass formoolar]
letter	der Brief [dair breef]
parcel	das Paket [dass pak-ayt]
post code	die Postleitzahl [dee posst-leit-zahl]
post office	das Postamt [dass posst-amt]
post/mail v	aufgeben [owf-gayben]
postage	das Porto [dass portoh]
postbox/mailbox	der Briefkasten [dair breef-kassten]
postcard	die Postkarte [dee posst-kartuh]
sender	der Absender [dair ap-zender]
stamp n	die Briefmarke [dee breef-markuh]
stamp v	frankieren [frankeeren]
weight	das Gewicht [dass ge-visht]

ON THE PHONE

I'd like...	Ich möchte bitte … [ish mershtuh bituh]
a phone card.	eine Telefonkarte. [einuh tay-lay-fohn-kartuh]
to reverse the charges.	ein R-Gespräch führen. [ein air-ge-shpresh fuuren]
an international telephone card, please.	eine internationale Telefonkarte. [einuh inter-nat-see-oh-nah-luh tay-lay-fohn-kartuh]
What's the national/ area code for...?	Wie ist die Vorwahl von …? [vee isst dee for-vahl fon]
I'd like to phone...	Ich möchte nach … telefonieren. [ish mershtuh nahkh … tay-lay-foh-neeren]
How much does it cost per minute?	Wie viel kostet es pro Minute? [vee feel kosstet ess proh mee-noo-tuh]
This is... speaking.	Hier spricht … [heer shprisht]
Hello, who's speaking?	Hallo, mit wem spreche ich? [haloh, mit vaym shpreshuh ish]
Can I speak to Mr/Mrs..., please?	Kann ich bitte Herrn/Frau … sprechen? [kan ish bituh hairn/frow … shpreshen]

answer the phone	abnehmen [ap-naymen]
(phone)call	der Anruf [dair anroof]
call v	anrufen [an-roofen]
charge	die Gebühr [dee ge-buur]
charger	das Ladekabel [dass lah-duh-kahbel]
connection n	die Verbindung [dee fair-bindung]
dial v	wählen [vaylen]
directory enquiries	die Auskunft [dee owss-kunft]
engaged	besetzt [be-zetst]
international call	das Auslandsgespräch [dass owss-lants-ge-shpresh]
line	das Telefongespräch [dass tay-lay-fohn-ge-shpresh]
local call	das Ortsgespräch [dass orts-ge-shpresh]
long-distance call	das Ferngespräch [dass fairn-ge-shpresh]
make a phone call	telefonieren [tay-lay-foh-neeren]
mobile phone	das Mobiltelefon [dass moh-beel-tay-lay-fohn], das Handy [dass hendee]
national/area code	die Vorwahlnummer [dee for-vahl-num-er]
payphone	der Münzfernsprecher [dert muunts-fairn-shpresher]
phone box	die Telefonzelle [dee tay-lay-fohn-tseluh]
phone call/conversation	das Gespräch [dass ge-shpresh]
phone card	die Telefonkarte [dee tay-lay-fohn-kartuh]
phone number	die Telefonnummer [dee tay-lay-fohn-num-er]
prepaid card	die Prepaid-Karte [dee pree-payt-kartuh]
reverse-charge/collect call	das R-Gespräch [dass air-ge-shpresh]
SIM card	die SIM-Karte [dee zim-kartuh]

smartphone	das Smartphone [dass smart-fohn]
telephone	das Telefon [dass tay-lay-fohn]
telephone directory	das Telefonbuch [dass tay-lay-fohn-bookh]

■MOBILE PHONE | HANDY [hendee]

There's nothing left on my prepaid card.	Meine Prepaid-Karte ist leer. [meinuh pree-payt-kartuh isst lair]
I'd like to top up my card.	Ich möchte meine Karte aufladen. [ish mershtuh meinuh kartuh owf-lahden]
A prepaid card (for [network provider]), please.	Bitte eine Prepaid-Karte (von …). [bituh einuh pree-payt-kartuh …]
How much call time do I get with a card for... [amount of money]?	Wie viele Minuten kann ich mit einer Karte für … sprechen? [vee feeluh mee-noo-ten kan ish mit einer kartuh fuur … shpreshen]
What region is this SIM card valid for?	Für welches Gebiet gilt diese SIM-Karte? [fuur velshess ge-beet gilt deezuh zim-kartuh]
Please give me a price list/ the tarif information.	Könnten Sie mir bitte eine Tarifübersicht geben? [kernten zee meer bituh einuh tareef-uuber-zisht gayben]
Have you got prepaid cards for [network provider]?	Haben Sie auch Prepaid-Karten von …? [hahben zee owkh pree-payt-karten fon]
My battery's empty. Do you have a charger I could use?	Mein Akku ist leer. Haben Sie ein Ladekabel für mich? [mein ak-oo isst lair hahben zee ein lah-duh-kahbel fuur mish]

TAKING PHOTOS

 Point & Show: page 59

Do you mind if I take a picture of you?	Darf ich Sie fotografieren? [darf ish zee foh-toh-graf-eeren]
Am I allowed to take pictures here?	Ist hier Fotografieren erlaubt? [isst heer foh-toh-graf-eeren air-lowpt]
Would you mind taking a photo of us?	Wären Sie wohl so freundlich, ein Foto von uns zu machen? [vayren zee vohl zoh froynt-lish, ein fohtoh fon unss tsoo makhen]
Just press this button.	Drücken Sie bitte auf diesen Knopf. [druuken zee bituh owf deezen knopf]
That's very kind.	Das ist sehr freundlich (of you = von Ihnen). [dass isst zair froynt-lish (fon eenen)]

POLICE

Where's the nearest police station, please?	Wo ist bitte das nächste Polizeirevier? [voh isst bituh dass naykss-tuh poh-leets-ei-ray-veer]
I'd like to report...	Ich möchte … anzeigen. [ish mershtuh … an-tseigen]
a theft.	einen Diebstahl [einen deep-shtahl]
a loss.	einen Verlust [einen fair-lusst]
an accident.	einen Unfall [einen un-fal]
I've been mugged/raped.	Ich bin überfallen/vergewaltigt worden. [ish bin uuber-falen/fair-ge-val-tisht vorden]
My...	Mir ist … [meer isst]
handbag/	meine Handtasche [meinuh hant-tashuh]/
wallet/	mein Geldbeutel [mein gelt-boytel]/
camera/	mein Fotoapparat [mein foh-toh-apa-raht]/
car...	mein Auto … [mein owtoh]
has been stolen.	gestohlen worden. [ge-shtoh-len vorden]
My car has been broken into.	Mein Auto ist aufgebrochen worden. [mein owtoh isst owf-gebrokhen vorden]
I've lost...	Ich habe … verloren. [ish hahbuh … fair-lohren]
My son/daughter is missing.	Mein Sohn/Meine Tochter ist verschwunden. [mein zohn/meinuh tokhter isst fair-shvunden]
Can you help me, please?	Können Sie mir bitte helfen? [kernen zee meer bituh helfen]
I'd like to speak to a lawyer.	Ich möchte einen Anwalt sprechen. [ish mershtuh einen an-valt shpreshen]
Please get in touch with the...	Wenden Sie sich bitte an das … [venden zee zish bituh an dass …]
British/	britische [brit-ish-uh]/
U.S./	amerikanische [amair-ee-kahn-ish-uh]/
Irish/	irische [eer-ish-uh]/
Canadian consulate.	kanadische Konsulat. [kan-ah-dish-uh kon-soo-laht]

arrest v	verhaften [fairhaften]
attack n	der Überfall [dair uuber-fal]
bank card	die Scheckkarte [dee shek-kartuh]
beat up v	zusammenschlagen [tsoo-zam-en-shlah-gen]
break into/open	aufbrechen [owf-breshen]
car radio	das Autoradio [dass owtoh-radee-oh]
car key	der Autoschlüssel [dair owtoh-shluussel]
cheque/check	der Scheck [dair shek]
confiscate	beschlagnahmen [beshlahk-nahmen]
court	das Gericht [dass ge-risht]
crime	das Verbrechen [dass fair-breshen]
documents	Papiere nt [papeeruh]
drugs	das Rauschgift [dass rowsh-gift], Drogen pl/f [drohgen]

harass	belästigen [be-less-tig-en]
identity card	der Personalausweis [dair pair-zohnahl-owss-veiss]
judge	der Richter [dair rishter], die Richterin [dee rishter-in]
key	der Schlüssel [dair shluussel]
lawyer	der Rechtsanwalt [dair reshts-an-valt], die Rechtsanwältin [dee reshts an-velt-in]
lose	verlieren [fairleeren]
money	das Geld [dass gelt]
papers	Papiere nt [papeeruh]
passport	der Reisepass [dair reizuh-pass]
pickpocket	der Taschendieb [dair tashen-deep]
police	die Polizei [dee poh-lee-tsei]
policeman/policewoman	der Polizist [dair poh-lee-tsisst], die Polizistin [dee poh-lee-tsiss-tin]
prison	das Gefängnis [dass ge-feng-niss]
purse	der Geldbeutel [dair gelt-boytel]
rape n	die Vergewaltigung [dee fair-gevaltigung]
report v	anzeigen [an-tseigen]
theft	der Diebstahl [dair deep-shtahl]
thief	der Dieb [dair deep]
wallet	die Brieftasche [dee breef-tashuh]

TOILETS & BATHROOMS

Where is the toilet, please?	Wo ist bitte die Toilette? [voh isst bituh dee twa-let-uh]
May I use your toilet?	Dürfte ich wohl bei Ihnen die Toilette benutzen? [duurftuh ish vohl bei eenen dee twa-let-uh benut-sen]
Could you give me the key for the toilets, please?	Würden Sie mir bitte den Schlüssel für die Toiletten geben? [vuurden zee meer bituh dayn shluussel fuur dee twa-let-en gayben]
The toilet is blocked.	Die Toilette ist verstopft. [dee twa-let-uh isst fair-shtopft]

clean adj	sauber [zowber]
dirty	schmutzig [shmut-sish]
Gents (toilet for men)	(die) Herren(toilette) [(dee) hairen(twa-let-uh)]
Ladies (toilet for women)	(die) Damen(toilette) [(dee) dahmen(twa-let-uh)]
soap	die Seife [dee zei-fuh]
toilet paper	das Toilettenpapier [dass twa-let-en-pap-eer]

| towel | das Handtuch [dass hant-tookh] |
| washbasin | das Waschbecken [dass vash-bek-en] |

TRAVELLING WITH KIDS

Do you have children's portions?	Gibt es auch Kinderportionen? [geept ess owkh kinder-port-see-ohnen]
Could you warm up the bottle, please?	Könnten Sie mir bitte das Fläschchen warm machen? [kernten zee meer bituh dass flesh-shen varm makhen]
Do you have a baby changing room?	Haben Sie einen Wickelraum? [hahben zee einen vik-el-rowm]
Where can I breastfeed my baby?	Wo kann ich stillen? [voh kahn en ish shtil-en]
Please bring another high chair.	Bitte bringen Sie noch einen Kinderstuhl. [bituh bringen zee nokh einen kinder-shtool]

armbands/water wings	Schwimmflügel pl/m [dair shvim-fluugel]
baby changing table	der Wickeltisch [dair vik-el-tish]
baby food	die Kindernahrung [dee kinder-nahrung]
baby monitor	das Babyfon [dass baybee-fohn]
babysitter	der Babysitter [dair bay-bee-zit-er]
bottle warmer	der Fläschchenwärmer [dair flesh-shen-vairmer]
child discount	die Kinderermäßigung [dee kinder air-may-si-gung]
child's safety seat	der Kinderautositz [dair kinder owtoh-zits]
cot	das Babybett [dass baybee-bet]
day care	die Kinderbetreuung [dee kinder-be-troy-ung]
dummy	der Schnuller [dair shnul-er]
feeding bottle	die Saugflasche [dee zowk-flashuh]
nappies/diapers	Windeln f [vindeln]
paddling pool	das Planschbecken [dass plansh-bek-en]
playground	der Spielplatz [dair shpeel-plats]
rubber ring	der Schwimmring [dair shvim-ring]
toys	Spielsachen pl [shpeel-zakhen]

> Weather: page 19
> Numbers: Inside front cover
> Time: page 16, 17

THE MOST IMPORTANT WORDS

The numbers printed after some words are there to point you to the relevant page in a related chapter.

Abbreviations used: adj = adjective; adv = adverb; n = noun; prep = preposition; v = verb; Am: = American English; Br: = British English; sing = singular; pl = plural

A

a ein m/nt [ein], eine f [einuh]
abandon verlassen [fair-lassen]
able: to be able to können [kernen]
about ungefähr [un-ge-fair], etwa [et-va]; (time, e.g. about 7pm) gegen [gaygen]
absolutely unbedingt [un-be-dinkt]
accessible (for people with disabilities) behindertengerecht [be-hin-der-ten-ge-resht]
accident der Unfall [dair un-fal] ➤ 25, das Unglück [dass un-gluuk]
accident: to have an accident verunglücken [fair-un-gluuk-en]
accommodation die Unterkunft [dee unter-kunft]
accompany begleiten [be-glei-ten]
activity die Aktivität [dee ak-tee-vee-tayt]
activity holiday/vacation der Aktivurlaub [dair ak-teef-oor-lowp] ➤ 85
additional zusätzlich [tsoo-zets-lish]
address n die Adresse [dee a-dress-uh] ➤ 114; die Anschrift [dee an-shrift]
addressee der Empfänger [dair emp-fenger] ➤ 114
adjust richtigstellen [rish-tish-shtel-en]; (clothes) ändern [en-dairn]
adult n ein Erwachsener [ein air-vakss-en-er], eine Erwachsene [einuh air-vakss-en-uh]
advance booking der Vorverkauf [dair for-fair-kowf] ➤ 83
advance: in advance im Voraus [im fohr-owss]
advise raten [rah-ten], beraten [be-rah-ten]
aeroplane (airplane) das Flugzeug [dass flook-tsoyk] ➤ 29
afraid: to be afraid of sich fürchten vor [zish fuursh-ten for]
after nach [nahkh], danach [da-nahkh]
afternoon der Nachmittag [dair nahkh-mit-ahk]; in the afternoon nachmittags [nahkh-mit-ahkss]
again wieder [veeder], noch (ein~)mal [nokh (ein~)mahl]; **against** gegen [gaygen]
age n das Alter [dass al-ter] ➤ 14
agency (office, bureau) das Amt [dass amt]
agree (to agree to) zustimmen [tsoo-shtim-en]; (to agree on/about) sich einigen [zish ein-igen], vereinbaren [fair-ein-bah-ren]
air die Luft [dee luft]
airport der Flughafen [dair flook-hah-fen]

alcohol level (blood) die Promille [dee proh-mil-uh]
all alle [al-uh]
allow erlauben [air-low-ben]; to be allowed dürfen [duur-fen]
alone allein [al-ein]
along prep entlang [ent-lang]
already schon [shohn]
also auch [owkh]
altitude die Höhe [dee her-huh]
always immer [im-er]
ambulance der Krankenwagen [dair kranken-vahgen]
American (man/woman) der Amerikaner [dair am-air-ee-kah-ner], die Amerikanerin [dee am-air-ee-kahn-er-in]
among unter [unter], zwischen [tsvish-en]
among others unter anderem [unter ander-em]
amount (money) der Betrag [dair be-trahk], die Summe [dee zum-uh] ➤ 106
and und [unt]
angry verärgert [fair air-gert], böse [ber-zuh], zornig [tsorn-ish]
animal das Tier [dass teer]
annoy belästigen [be-less-tig-en] ➤ 118
annoyed: to be annoyed about/at sich ärgern über [zish air-gern uuber]
annoying ärgerlich [air-ger-lish], lästig [less-tish]
another ein anderer/eine andere/ein anderes m/f/nt [ein ander-er/einuh ander-uh/ ein ander-ess]; (another (drink, etc.)) noch ein/e/r nt/f/m [nokh ein/-uh/-er]
apart from außerdem [owss-er-daym]
apartment die Wohnung [dee voh-nung]
apologize sich entschuldigen [zish ent-shuld-igen] ➤ 12
appetite der Appetit [dair ap-ay-teet]
appointment (meeting) der Termin [dair tair-meen], die Verabredung [dee fair-ap-ray-dung] ➤ 15
area code die Vorwahlnummer [dee for-vahl-num-er] ➤ 115
around prep um [um]
arrival die Ankunft [dee an-kunft] ➤ 30, 31
arrive ankommen [an-kom-en] ➤ 32
as far as I'm concerned meinerseits [mei-ner-zeits]
as if als ob [alss op]
ask fragen [frah-gen]; **ask s.o. for sth** jdn um etw bitten [yay-man-den um et-vass bit-en]
at (time) um [um]
at home daheim [da-heim]

at least mindestens [min-dess-tenss]
attack n der Angriff [dair an-grif]
aunt die Tante [dee tan-tuh]
authorities (police, etc.) die Behörde [dee be-her-duh]
available (on sale) erhältlich [air-helt-lish]
average n das Mittel [dass mit-el]; adj durchschnittlich [doorsh-shnit-lish]; **on average** im Durchschnitt [im doorsh-shnit]
awake adj wach [vakh]
away (gone) fort [fort], weg [vek]

B

baby das Baby [dass baybee] > 119
bachelor der Junggeselle [dair yung-ge-zeluh]
back (i.e. to be back) zurück [tsoo-ruuk]
bad/badly schlecht [shlesht]
ball (sports) der Ball [dair bal]; (dance) der Ball [dair bal]
band (music) die Band [dee bant], die (Musik~)Kapelle [dee moozeek~]kap-el-uh]
bank die Bank [dee bank] > 104
bar die Bar [dee bar], die Kneipe [dee knei-puh] > 82
bathing/seaside resort der Badeort [dair bah-duh-ort]
bay (sea, etc.) die Bucht [dee bukht]
be v sein [zein]
beach der Strand [dair shtrant] > 84
beautiful schön [shern]
because weil [veil], denn [den]; **because of** wegen [vaygen]
become werden [vair-den]
bed das Bett [dass bet]
bedroom das Zimmer [dass tsim-er] > 6, 74
bee die Biene [dee bee-nuh]
before vor [for]
begin beginnen [beg-in-en]
beginning der Anfang [dair an-fang]
behind hinter [hinter]
believe glauben [glow-ben]
bell die Klingel [dee kling-el]
belong gehören [ge-her-ren]
below unter [unter], unterhalb [unter-halp]
bench die (Sitz~)Bank [dee (zits~)bank]
bend (in a road, etc.) die Kurve [dee kur-vuh]
beside/by prep neben [nayben], nahe bei [nahuh bei]
between zwischen [tsvish-en]
bicycle das Fahrrad [dass far-raht] > 23, 87
big groß [grohss]
bill (Am: the check) die Rechnung [dee resh-nung]
birth die Geburt [dee ge-boort]
birthday der Geburtstag [dair ge-burts-tahk] > 12
birthplace der Geburtsort [dair ge-boorts-ort]
bite v beißen [beiss-en]
black schwarz [shvarts]
blanket die (Bett~)Decke [dee (bet~)dek-uh]

blood das Blut [dass bloot] > 109
blue blau [blow]
boat das Boot [dass boht] > 85
body der Körper [dair ker-per] > 109
boil v kochen [kokhen]
book das Buch [dass bookh]
booking die Buchung [dee bookh-ung] > 6, 30, 83
border die Grenze [dee gren-tsuh] > 22
boring langweilig [lang-veil-ish]
born geboren [ge-bor-en]
boss der Chef [dair shef], die Chefin [dee shef-in]
both beide [bei-duh]
bottle die Flasche [dee flash-uh]
bouquet der (Blumen~)Strauß [dair (bloomen~)shtrowss]
boy der Junge [dair yung-uh]
boyfriend der Freund [dair froynt]
brakes n die Bremse [dee brem-zuh] > 24
brand (i.e. brand name) die Marke [dee mar-kuh]
bread das Brot [dass broht] > 43, 46, 63
break brechen [bresh-en]; (to break open/into) aufbrechen [owf-breshen] > 117
breakdown (car, etc.) die Panne [dee pan-uh] > 24, 25
breakfast das Frühstück [dass fruu-shtuuk] > 46, 70
brief adj kurz [kurts]
bring bringen [bringen]; (to bring along with) mitbringen [mit-bringen]
broad breit [breit]
broken kaputt [ka-put]
brother der Bruder [dair brooder]
brother-in-law der Schwager [dair shvah-ger]
building das Gebäude [dass ge-boy-duh] > 80
bureau de change die Wechselstube [dee vekssel-shtoo-buh] > 104
burn v brennen [bren-en]
bus der Bus [dair buss] > 34
business days werktags [vairk-tahkss]; sing der Werktag [dair vairk-tahk]
but aber [ahber]
buy v kaufen [kowfen]
by (i.e. written by) von [fon]
bye! tschüss! [tshuuss]

C

cabin die Kabine [dee ka-bee-nuh] > 33
café das Café [dass kafay]
calculate rechnen [reshnen]
calendar of events der Veranstaltungskalender [dair fair-an-shtal-tungss-kal-en-der]
call v rufen [roofen]; (on the phone) anrufen [an-roofen], telefonieren [tay-lay-foh-nee-ren]
called: to be called heißen [heiss-en], sich nennen [zish nen-en]
calm n die Ruhe [dee roo-uh]; (calm down) sich beruhigen [zish be-roo-igen]
camping das Camping [dass kemping] > 76

campsite der Campingplatz [dair kemping-plats]

Canada Kanada [kanadah]

Canadian (man/woman) der Kanadier [ka-nah-dee-er], die Kanadierin [ka-nah-dee-er-in]

cancel stornieren [shtor-nee-ren]; (tickets) abbestellen [ap-be-shtel-en] ➤ 29

capable: to be capable of imstande sein [im-shtan-duh zein]

car das Auto [dass owtoh] ➤ 23

care: take care of sich kümmern um [zish kuum-ern um], sorgen für [zorgen fuur]

carry tragen [trahgen]

cash n das Bargeld [dass bar-gelt]

cash register die Kasse [dee kassuh]

cashpoint (ATM) der Geldautomat [dair gelt owtoh-maht] ➤ 105

castle (defensive) die Burg [dee burk]; (residential) das Schloss [dass shloss] ➤ 80

cat die Katze [dee kat-suh]

caution n (care) die Vorsicht [dee for-zisht]

ceiling die (Zimmer~)Decke [dee (tsim-er~)dekuh]

celebration das Fest [dass fesst]

cell phone (Br: mobile phone) das Handy [dass hendee] ➤ 115

centre (Am: center) das Zentrum [dass tsen-trum]

certain/certainly bestimmt [be-shtimt], gewiss [ge-viss]

certify bescheinigen [be-shein-igen]

chair der Stuhl [dair shtool]

change n (coins) das Kleingeld [dass klein-gelt] ➤ 106

change v ändern [en-dern], verändern [vair-en-dern]; (a booking) umbuchen [um-bookhen] ➤ 39; (trains) umsteigen [um-shtei-gen]

channel (TV) der Kanal [dair kanahl]

chapel die Kapelle [dee ka-pel-uh] ➤ 80

cheap billig [bil-ish]

cheat v betrügen [be-truu-gen]

check n (Br: the bill) die Rechnung [dee resh-nung]

check v kontrollieren [kon-tro-lee-ren], nachprüfen [nahkh-pruufen]

cheerful froh [froh], heiter [heiter]

cheese der Käse [dair kay-zuh] ➤ 43, 50, 63

chemist's/drugstore die Drogerie [dee droh-geree]

cheque (Am: check) der Scheck [dair shek] ➤ 106

child das Kind [dass kint]

choose wählen [vaylen]

church die Kirche [dee kirsh-uh] ➤ 80

cigarette die Zigarette [dee tsee-ga-ret-uh]

cinema das Kino [dass kee-noh] ➤ 83

city centre die Innenstadt [dee in-en-shtat]

city hall das Rathaus [dass raht-howss] ➤ 80

clean v putzen [put-sen], reinigen [rein-igen]; adj sauber [zowber]

clergyman/woman der Geistliche [dair geisst-lish-uh], die Geistliche [dee geisst-lish-uh]

clever (intelligent) klug [kloog]

climate das Klima [dass klee-mah]

climb v steigen [shtei-gen], klettern [klet-ern]

clock die Wanduhr [dee vant-oor]

closed geschlossen [ge-shloss-en]

clothes die Kleidung [dee klei-dung] ➤ 62

club (night club) der Club [dair klup], die Diskothek [dee diss-koh-tayk]

coast die Küste [dee kuuss-tuh]

coffee der Kaffee [dair kafay] ➤ 46, 53, 63

coin das Geldstück [dass gelt-shtuuk], die Münze [dee muunt-suh]

cold adj kalt [kalt]

collect v sammeln [zam-eln]

colour n (Am: color) die Farbe [dee far-buh]

come in! herein! [hair-ein]

come v kommen [kom-en]; (come from/originate) stammen aus [shtam-en owss]

common adj (shared) gemeinsam [ge-mein-zahm]; (frequent) häufig [hoy-fish]; (general) allgemein [al-ge-mein]

company (business) die Firma [dee fir-mah]

compare v vergleichen [fair-gleish-en]

compensation (for damages) die Entschädigung [dee ent-shay-di-gung]

complain (about) sich beklagen (über) [zish be-klah-gen (uuber)]; (more formal) sich beschweren (über) [zish be-shvair-en (uuber)], reklamieren [ray-kla-mee-ren] ➤ 38, 70

complaint die Beanstandung [dee be-an-shtan-dung] ➤ 38, 70

complete/completely ganz [gants], vollständig [fol-shten-dish], vollkommen [fol-kom-en],

compliments die Komplimente nt, pl [dee kom-plee-men-tuh] ➤ 13

computer der Computer [dair komp-yoo-ter]

computer shop/store die Computerhandlung [dee komp-yoo-ter-hand-lung] ➤ 56, 59

concert das Konzert [dass kon-tsairt] ➤ 83

concierge (porter) der Portier [dair por-tee-ay]

condom das Kondom [dass kon-dohm]

confirm bestätigen [be-shtay-ti-gen]

confiscate beschlagnahmen [be-shlahk-nah-men]

confuse verwechseln [fair-vek-seln]

congratulate gratulieren [grat-oo-leer-en]

congratulations der Glückwunsch [dair gluuk-vunsh] ➤ 12

connect (technology, etc.) verbinden [fair-bin-den]

connection (personal) die Verbindung [dee fair-bin-dung]; (travel) der Anschluss [dair an-shluss] ➤ 30, 32

constitution (political) die (Staats~)Verfassung [dee (shtah-tss~)fair-fass-ung]

consulate das Konsulat [dass kon-zoo-laht]

contact n der Kontakt [dair kontakt], v kontaktieren [kontakt-ee-ren]

contents der Inhalt [dair in-halt]

continue fortsetzen [fort-zet-sen]
contraceptive das Verhütungsmittel [dass fair-huut-ungss-mit-el]
contract n der Vertrag [dair fair-trahk]
conversation das Gespräch [dass ge-shpraysh], die Unterhaltung [dee unter-haltung]
cook v kochen [kokhen]
cool (temp.) kühl [kuul]
corner die Ecke [dee ek-uh]
corrupt adj verdorben [fair-dor-ben]
cost v kosten [koss-ten]
counter (post office, etc.) der Schalter [dair shal-ter] **>** 106, 114
country (nation) das Land [dass lant]; (home/native country) die Heimat [dee hei-maht]
couple (married) das Ehepaar [dass ay-uh-par]
course (lessons) der Kurs [dair kurss]; (meal) der Gang [dair gang]
court (law) das Gericht [dass ge-risht] **>** 117
cousin der Cousin [dair koo-zañ], die Cousine [dee koo-zee-nuh]
credit card die Kreditkarte [dee kray-deet-kartuh] **>** 54, 106
criticize v kritisieren [kree-tee-zee-ren]
cross (a road, etc.) überqueren [uuber-kvair-en]
cry (weep) weinen [vei-nen]
culture die Kultur [dee kul-toor]
curious (interested) neugierig [noy-geer-ish]
currency die Währung [dee vay-rung] **>** 106
current (electrical) der Strom [dair shtrohm]
cushion das Kissen [dass kissen]
customs (border control) der Zoll [dair tsol] **>** 22
customs duty die Zollgebühren [dee tsol-ge-buuren]
customs office das Zollamt [dass tsol-amt]
customs officer der Zollbeamte [dair tsol-buh-am-tuh], die Zollbeamtin [dee tsol-buh-am-tin]
cut v schneiden [shnei-den]
cutlery (silverware) das Besteck [dass be-shtek]
cycle v Rad fahren [raht fahren] **>** 23, 87

D

damage n der Schaden [dair shah-den]; v schaden [shah-den], beschädigen [be-shay-di-gen]
damaged (faulty, defective) defekt [day-fekt] **>** 24
dance v tanzen [tant-sen] **>** 82
dangerous gefährlich [ge-fair-lish]
dark dunkel [dun-kel]
date n (appointment) die Verabredung [dee fair-ap-ray-dung]; (calendar) das Datum **>** 17 [dass dah-tum]; (date of birth) das Geburtsdatum [dass ge-boorts-dah-tum] **>** 22
daughter die Tochter [dee tokh-ter]
day der Tag [dair tahk]; (day of arrival) der Anreisetag [dair an-rei-zuh-tahk]
dead tot [toht]
dear (friend, etc.) lieb [leep]

death der Tod [dair toht]
debt die Schuld [dee shuld]
decide entscheiden [ent-shei-den]
decision der Entschluss [dair ent-shluss]
declare erklären [air-klair-en]
deep tief [teef]
definite/definitely endgültig [ent-guul-tish]
degree (temperature, etc.) Grad m [graht]
demand v fordern [for-dern]
denomination (relig.) die Konfession [dee kon-fess-ee-ohn]
dentist der Zahnarzt [dair tsahn-artst] **>** 108
departure die Abfahrt [dee ap-fart], die Abreise [dee ap-rei-zuh]
deposit (for bottles, etc.) das Pfand [dass pfant]; (security deposit) die Kaution [dee kow-tsee-ohn] **>** 74
deserve verdienen [fair-dee-nen]
destination das (Reise~)Ziel [dass (reizuh~)tseel]
destroy zerstören [tsair-shter-ren]
details (personal details) die Personalien [dee pair-zohn-ahl-ee-en]
develop entwickeln [ent-vik-eln]
dial (phone number) wählen [vay-len]
die sterben [shtair-ben]
difference der Unterschied [dair unter-sheet]
different adj unterschiedlich [unter-sheet-lish], verschieden [fair-shee-den]
differently adv anders [anderss]
difficult schwierig [shveer-ish]
direction die Richtung [dee rish-tung]
director (manager) der Direktor [dair dee-rek-tor]
directory das Verzeichnis [dass fair-tseish-niss]
dirt n der Schmutz [dair shmuts]
dirty adj schmutzig [shmuts-ish]
disabled toilets die Behindertentoilette [dee be-hin-der-ten-twa-let-uh]
disappointed enttäuscht [ent-toysht]
disco die Diskothek [dee diss-koh-tayk] **>** 83
discount der Rabatt [dair ra-bat]
discover entdecken [ent-dek-en]
distance die Strecke [dee shtre-kuh]
distant (far away) entfernt [ent-fairnt]
distrust (something/someone) (etw/jdm) misstrauen [(et-vass/yay-man-dem) miss-trow-en]
disturb stören [shter-ren]
disturbance die Störung [dee shter-rung]
diversion die Umleitung [dee um-leit-ung]
dizzy adj schwindlig [shvint-lish]
dizziness n der Schwindel [dair shvin-del]
do v machen [makhen], tun [toon]
doctor (medical) der Arzt [dair artst], die Ärztin [dee airts-tin]; (academic) der Doktor [dair doktor], die Doktorin [dee doktor-in] **>** 107
dog der Hund [dair hunt], die Hündin [dee huun-din]
door die Tür [dee tuur]

double doppelt [dop-elt]

doubt sth an etw zweifeln [an et-vass tsveif-eln]

downwards abwärts [ap-vairts]

dream v träumen [troy-men]

dress (a wound) verbinden [fair-bind-en]

dressing n der Verband [dair fair-bant]

drink n das Getränk [dass ge-trenk] **> 38, 45, 51, 52;** v trinken [trinken]

drive v fahren [fah-ren]

driving licence der Führerschein [dair fuurer-shein]; (car documents) Autopapiere [owtoh-papeeruh]

drunk adj betrunken [be-trunken]; (to get drunk) sich betrinken [zish be-trinken]

duration die Dauer [dee dow-er]

during während [vay-rent]

duty die Pflicht [dee pflisht]

E

e-mail address die E-Mail-Adresse [dee ee-mayl-adress-uh]

early früh [fruu]

earn verdienen [fair-dee-nen]

earth die Erde [dee air-duh]

east der Osten [dair oss-ten]

easy leicht [leisht], einfach [ein-fakh]

eat essen [essen] **> 36, 63**

edge der Rand [dair rant]

edible essbar [essbar]

education die Erziehung [dee air-tsee-ung]

effort (trouble) die Mühe [dee muu-uh]

egg das Ei [dass ei]

either...or entweder ... oder [ent-vay-der ... ohder]

electrical shop die Elektrohandlung [dee ay-lek-troh-hand-lung] **> 56, 59**

elevator der Fahrstuhl [dair far-shtool]

embassy die Botschaft [dee boht-shaft]

emergency brake die Notbremse [dee noht-brem-zuh]

emergency exit der Notausgang [dair noht-owss-gang]

emergency telephone die Notrufsäule [dee noht-roof-zoyluh]

emphasis die Betonung [dee be-toh-nung], der Ton [dair tohn]

employment die (An~)Stellung [dee (an-)shtel-ung]

empty leer [lair]

end v enden [enden]

engaged: to get engaged to sich mit jdn verloben [zish mit yay-man-den fair-lohben]

engine (motor) der Motor [dair mohtor] **> 24, 27**

England England [en-glant]

English englisch [en-glish]

English(~man/~woman) der Engländer [dair en-glender], die Engländerin [dee en-glender-in]

enjoy genießen [ge-nee-sen]

enough genug [ge-nook]

enquire sich erkundigen [zish air-kund-igen]

enter eintreten [ein-tray-ten], hereinkommen [hair-ein-kom-en]; (a country) einreisen [ein-reizen]

entertainment die Unterhaltung [dee unter-haltung] **> 82;** (entertaining) unterhaltsam [unter-halt-zahm]

entrance der Eingang [dair ein-gang]

environment die Umwelt [dee um-velt]

et cetera (etc.) und so weiter (usw.) [unt zoh vei-ter]

Euro der Euro [dair oy-roh] **> 104**

Europe Europa [oy-roh-pah]

European (man/woman) der Europäer [dair oy-roh-pay-er], die Europäerin [dee oy-roh-pay-er-in]

even adv sogar [zoh-gar]

evening der Abend [dair ahbent]

event (occurrence) das Ereignis [dass air-eik-niss]; (organised) die Veranstaltung [dee fair-an-shtal-tung]

every jeder [yay-der]; (every time) jedesmal [yay-dess-mahl]; (everyone) jedermann [yay-der-man]; (everywhere) überall [uuber-al]

evil böse [ber-zuh]

exact/exactly genau [ge-now]

examination (inspection/medical) die Untersuchung [dee unter-zookhung], die Prüfung [dee pruu-fung]; (school, etc.) die Prüfung [dee pruu-fung]

examine (inspect) prüfen [pruu-fen], untersuchen [unter-zookhen]

example das Beispiel [dass bei-shpeel]

except (apart from) außer [owsser]

exchange umtauschen [um-tow-shen]

exchange rate der (Wechsel~)Kurs [dair (vekssel-)kurss] **> 107**

excuse n die Entschuldigung [dee ent-shuldi-gung]

exhausted erschöpft [air-sherpft]

exit n der Ausgang [dair owss-gang]; (motorway/highway) die (Autobahn~)Ausfahrt [dee (owtohbahn-)owss-fart]

expenses die Unkosten [dee un-koss-ten]

expensive adj teuer [toyer]

experienced adj erfahren [air-fah-ren]

expire (voucher, etc.) ablaufen [ap-low-fen]

explain erklären [air-klair-en]

extend v verlängern [fair-len-gern]

extinguish löschen [ler-shen]

F

factory die Fabrik [dee fa-breek]

fair (event) die Messe [dee messuh]; (weather) heiter [hei-ter]

faith der Glaube [dair glow-buh]

faithful treu [troy]

fall v fallen [fal-en]

family die Familie [dee famee-lee-uh]

far (distance) weit [veit]

DICTIONARY

far away weit [veit (ent-fairnt)]
farewell: say farewell Abschied nehmen [ap-sheet nay-men] **> 12**
fashion die Mode [dee moh-duh] **> 62**
fast-food restaurant der Schnellimbiss [dair shnel-imbiss]
fat n das Fett [fet]; adj dick [dik]
father der Vater [dair fahter]
fear n die Angst [dee angsst]; v fürchten [fuursh-ten], befürchten [be-fuursh-ten]
fee die Gebühr [dee ge-buur]; (professional charge) das Honorar [dass hoh-noh-rar]
feel v fühlen [fuu-len]
feeling das Gefühl [dass ge-fuul]
female/feminine weiblich [veip-lish]
festival das Fest [dass fesst]
few wenig [vay-nish]; (a few) ein paar [ein par]
fiancé/fiancée der Verlobte [dair fair-lohp-tuh], die Verlobte [dee fair-lohp-tuh]
field das Feld [dass felt]
fill in/out (a form, etc.) ausfüllen [owss-fuu-len]
film n der Film [dair film] **> 83**
finally endlich [ent-lish]
find v finden [finden]
fine (financial penalty) die (Geld~)Strafe [dee (gelt~)shtrah-fuh]
finish beenden [buh-en-den]
finished fertig [fair-tish]
fire das Feuer [dass foyer]; (building, forest, etc.) der Brand [dair brant]
fire alarm der Feuermelder [dair foyer-melder]
fire extinguisher der Feuerlöscher [dair foyer-ler-sher]
fire service die Feuerwehr [dee foyer-vair]
firewood das Brennholz [dass bren-holts]
first aid die Erste Hilfe [dee airss-tuh hil-fuh]
first floor (Br: ground floor) das Erdgeschoss [dass airt-ge-shoss]
first name der Vorname [dair for-nah-muh] **> 22**
firstly (first of all) erst [airsst], zuerst [tsoo-airsst]
fish der Fisch [dair fish] **> 45, 47, 64**
fishmonger der Fischhändler [dair fish-hend-ler]
flash (photo) der Blitz [dair blits]
flat eben [ay-ben]
flaw (personality, etc.) der Fehler [dair fay-ler]
flight der Flug [dair flook] **> 29, 30**
flirt v flirten [flerten] **> 15**
floor (e.g. 1st floor) das Stockwerk [dass shtok-vairk]; (under foot) der (Fuß~)Boden [dair (fooss~)bohden]
flow v fließen [flee-sen]
flower die Blume [dee bloo-muh]
fly v fliegen [fleegen]; n die Fliege [dee flee-guh]
follow folgen [folgen]
food Lebensmittel nt [lay-bens-mit-el] **> 36, 63**
for für [fuur]; **to be for/pro sth** dafür sein [da-fuur zein]

forbid v verbieten [fair-bee-ten]
forbidden verboten [fair-boh-ten]
foreign fremd [fremt]; n (foreigner) der Ausländer [dair owss-lender], die Ausländerin [dee owss-lender-in], der Fremde [dair fremduh], die Fremde [dee fremduh]
forest der Wald [dair valt] **> 81**
forget v vergessen [fair-gessen]
forgive verzeihen [fair-tsei-en], vergeben [fair-gay-ben]
fork die Gabel [dee gah-bel]
form (to fill in) das Formular [dass for-moo-lar]
fragile zerbrechlich [tsair-bresh-lish]
free (of charge) umsonst [umzonsst]
freeze v frieren [freer-en]
French französisch [fran-tser-zish]
French(~man/~woman) der Franzose [dair fran-tsoh-zuh], die Französin [dee fran-tser-zin]
frequently häufig [hoy-fish]
fresh frisch [frish]
friend der Freund [dair froynt], die Freundin [dee froynd-in]
friendly freundlich [froynt-lish]
friends: to be friends befreundet sein [be-froyn-det zein]
frighten erschrecken [air-shrek-en]
from (origin) aus [owss], von [fon]; (time) ab [ap]
front: in front of vor [for]
fruit das Obst [dass oh-psst] **> 42, 46, 64**
full voll [fol], besetzt [be-zet-st]; (after food) satt [zat]
full board (accommodation) die Vollpension [dee fol-pen-zee-ohn] **> 70, 72**
fun n der Spaß [dair shpahss]; adj lustig [luss-tish]
furious wütend [vuu-tent]
furniture die Möbel nt, pl [dee merbel]
fuse (electric) die Sicherung [dee zisherung]

G

garage (for repairs) die (Reparatur~)Werkstatt [dee (ray-pa-ra-toor~)vairk-shtat] **> 24**; (for car storage) die Garage [dee ga-rah-zjuh]
garbage (Br: rubbish) der Müll [dair muul]
garden der Garten [dair gar-ten]
gas (Br: petrol) Benzin nt [bent-seen] **> 23**
gas station (Br: petrol station) die Tankstelle [dee tank-shteluh] **> 23, 27**
gear (on a car, etc.) der Gang [dair gang]
gentleman der Herr [dair hair]
genuine echt [esht]
German (man/woman) der Deutsche [dair doyt-shuh], die Deutsche [dee doyt-shuh]
Germany Deutschland [doyt-shlant]

get (obtain) besorgen [be-zorgen]
get out (of a bus, etc.) aussteigen
[owss-shteigen] ➤ 32, 34
get up aufstehen [owf-shtayen]
gift (present) das Geschenk [dass ge-shenk]
girl das Mädchen [dass mayt-shen]
girlfriend die Freundin [dee froynd-in]
give geben [gayben];
(as a present/gift) schenken [shenk-en]
give up: to give up aufgeben [owf-gayben]
gladly (with pleasure!) gern [gairn]
glasses (spectacles) die Brille [dee bril-uh] ➤ 65
glass (for drinking) das Glas [dass glahss];
(material) das Glas [dass glahss]
go v (on foot) gehen [gayen];
(in a vehicle) fahren [fahren]
goal (aim) das Ziel [dass tseel]
God Gott [got]
good gut [goot]
goodbye: to say goodbye sich verabschieden
[zish fair-ap-shee-den]
government die Regierung [dee ray-geer-ung]
grandfather, grandmother der Großvater [dair
grohss-fahter], die Großmutter [dee grohss-mut-er]
grandson, granddaughter der Enkel [dair en-kel],
die Enkelin [dee en-kel-in]
grave (tomb) das Grab [dass grahp]
great (important, significant) groß [grohss]
green grün [gruun]
greet grüßen [gruu-sen], begrüßen [be-gruu-sen]
grey grau [grow]
ground (earth) der Boden [dair boh-den]
ground floor (Am: first floor) das Erdgeschoss
[dass airt-ge-shoss]
group die Gruppe [dee grup-uh]
guarantee die Garantie [dee garantee]
guess raten [rah-ten], erraten [air-ah-ten]
guest der Gast [dair gasst]
guesthouse das Gasthaus [dass gasst-howss],
der Gasthof [dair gasst-hohf], die Pension
[dee pen-zee-ohn] ➤ 8, 68
guide (book) der Reiseführer [dair rei-zuh-fuu-rer]
➤ 67; (tour guide) der (Fremden~)Führer
[dair [frem-den-]fuu-rer]
guided tour die Führung [dee fuurung] ➤ 79
guilt die Schuld [dee shult]

H

hair das Haar [dass har] ➤ 61
hairdresser's der Friseur(~salon) [dair
freezuhr(~saloñ)] ➤ 56, 61
half halb [halp]
hall die Halle [dee hal-uh]
handwriting die (Hand~)Schrift [dee [hant-]shrift]
happen sich ereignen [zish air-eik-nen], geschehen
[ge-shayen], passieren [pass-eer-en]

happy glücklich [gluuk-lish]; (content, satisfied)
froh [froh], zufrieden [tsoo-freeden]
hard hart [hart]; (difficult) schwierig [shveer-ish]
hardly kaum [kowm]
harmful schädlich [shayt-lish]
have haben [hahben]
have to sollen [zol-en], müssen [muuss-en]
he er [air]
health die Gesundheit [dee ge-zunt-heit]
healthy gesund [ge-zunt]
hear hören [her-ren]
heating die Heizung [dee heit-sung] ➤ 70
heaven der Himmel [dair him-el]
heavy schwer [shvair]
Hello! Hallo! [hal-oh]
help n die Hilfe [dee hil-fuh];
(help s.o.) jdn helfen [(yay-man-den) hel-fen]
her ihr [eer]
here hier [heer]
high hoch [hoh-kh]
hike v (walk) wandern [van-dern] ➤ 87, 88
hill der Hügel [dair huugel]
hire mieten [meeten] 77;
(hire out) vermieten [fair-meeten]
his sein [zein]
history die Geschichte [dee ge-shish-tuh]
hobby das Hobby [dass hob-ee]
hold (fest~)halten [(fesst-)halten]
hole das Loch [dass lokh]
holiday (Am: vacation) die Ferien [dee fairee-en],
der Urlaub [dair oor-lowp]
holiday home das Ferienhaus
[dass fairee-en-howss] ➤ 9, 74
holy heilig [heil-ish]
home-made hausgemacht [howss-ge-makht]
hope v hoffen [hof-en]
hospital das Krankenhaus [dass kranken-howss]
➤ 108
host/hostess der Gastgeber [dair gasst-gayber],
die Gastgeberin [dee gasst-gayber-in]
hot heiß [heiss]
hotel das Hotel [dass hot-tel] ➤ 6, 68
hour die Stunde [dee shtun-duh]
house das Haus [dass howss]
household goods die Haushaltswaren pl
[dee hows-halts-vahren]
how? wie? [vee]
how long? wie lange? [vee languh]
how many? wie viele? [vee fee-luh]
how much? wie viel? [vee feel]
however doch [dokh], aber [ahber]
hug v umarmen [um-arm-en]
hunger (der) Hunger [(dair) hunger]
hungry hungrig [hung-rish]
hurt v schmerzen [shmairt-sen], wehtun [vay-toon]
husband der (Ehe~)Mann [dair (ayuh~)man]

DICTIONARY

I

I Ich [ish]

idea die Idee [dee eeday], die Ahnung [dee ahnung]; (concept) die Vorstellung [dee for-shtel-ung]; (I have no idea!) Ich habe keine Ahnung! [ish hahbuh keinuh ah-nung]

identity card (ID) der (Personal~)Ausweis [dair (pair-zohn-ahl~)owss-veiss]

if wenn [ven]

ill (Am: sick) krank [krank] > 110

illness die Krankheit [dee krank-heit] > 110

immediately gleich [gleish], sofort [zoh-fort]

impolite unhöflich [un-herf-lish]

import n die Einfuhr [dee ein-foor]

important wichtig [vish-tish]

impossible unmöglich [unmerk-lish]

in in [in]

in addition zusätzlich [tsoo-zets-lish]

included (in the price, etc.) inbegriffen [in-be-grif-en]

inform (about) informieren (über) [infor-mee-ren (uuber)], mitteilen [mit-teil-en]

information die Auskunft [dee owss-kunft]

information office/bureau die Auskunftstelle [dee owss-kunft-shteluh] > 56

inhabitant der Bewohner [dair be-vohner], die Bewohnerin [dee be-vohner-in]; der Einwohner [dair ein-vohner], die Einwohnerin [dee ein-vohner-in]

innocent unschuldig [un-shul-dish]

insect das Insekt [dass in-zekt]

inside adv innen [in-en], drin [drin], drinnen [drin-en]

inspect (check) nachsehen [nahkh-zayen], prüfen [pruu-fen]

instead of statt [shtat], anstatt [an-shtat]

insult v beleidigen [be-lei-dig-en]

insurance die Versicherung [dee fair-zisher-ung]

interested: to be interested (in) sich interessieren (für) [zish inter-ess-eer-en (fuur)]

international international [inter-nat-see-oh-nahl]

Internet das Internet [dass internet]

interrupt unterbrechen [unter-breshen]

interruption die Unterbrechung [dee unter-breshung]; (of work, etc.) die Störung [dee shter-rung]

introduction (person) die Vorstellung [dee for-shtel-ung]

invalid (void) ungültig [un-guul-tish]

invite einladen [ein-lah-den]

invoice amount (billing amount) der Rechnungsbetrag [dair resh-nungss-be-trahk]

Ireland, Eire Irland [ir-lant]

Irish (~man/~woman) der Ire [dair eeruh], die Irin [dee eer-in]

island die Insel [dee in-zel]

...isn't it? ... nicht wahr? [nisht var]

J

jellyfish die Qualle [dee kval-uh]

jewellery der Schmuck [dair shmuk] > 65

job (position) die (Arbeits~)Stelle [dee (arbeits~)shteluh]

joke n der Scherz [dair shairts]

journey n die Reise [dee rei-zuh], die Fahrt [dee fart]; (return journey) die Heimreise [dee heim-rei-zuh]

joy die Freude [dee froy-duh]

judge v urteilen [oor-tei-len]

just (a moment ago) eben [ay-ben]

just as... (good) as genau so ... (gut) wie [ge-now zoh ... (goot) vee]

K

keep halten [halten], behalten [be-halten]

key der Schlüssel [dair shluu-sel]

kind adj nett [net], liebenswürdig [lee-benss-vuur-dish]

kindness die Freundlichkeit [dee froynt-lish-keit]

kiss n der Kuss [dair kuss]; v küssen [kuussen]

kitchen die Küche [dee kuushuh]

knife das Messer [dass messer]

know v (a fact) wissen [vissen]; (to be familiar with) kennen [ken-en]

know: get to know s.o. jdn kennenlernen [yay-manden ken-en-lair-nen]

L

lack der Mangel [dair mangel]

ladder die Leiter [dee leiter]

lady die Dame [dee dahmuh]

lake der See [dair zay]

land (ground) das Land [dass lant]

landlord/landlady der Hausherr [dair howss-hair], die Hausherrin [dee howss-hair-in]; der Hausbesitzer [dair howss-be-zit-ser]/die Hausbesitzerin [dee howss-be-zit-ser-in] > 74; der Wirt [dair virt], die Wirtin [dee virt-in]

landscape die Landschaft [dee lant-shaft]

language die Sprache [dee shprah-khuh]

large groß [grohss]

last v dauern [dow-ern]

last (e.g. last place) letzte f [let-stuh], letzter m [let-ster], letztes nt [let-stess]

late spät [shpayt]; (to be late) sich verspäten [zish fair-shpay-ten]

later später [shpayter]

laugh v lachen [lakhen]

lawn der Rasen [dair rahzen]

lazy faul [fowl]

learn (become aware of) erfahren [air-fah-ren]

leave v verlassen [fair-lassen]; (go away) weggehen [vek-gayen]; (to leave for...) nach ... abreisen [nahkh ... ap-reizen]

left: on the left links [linkss]

126 | 127

lend leihen [lei-en]

length (measure, distance) die Länge [dee leng-uh]

less weniger [vay-nig-er]

let (allow) (zu~)lassen [(tsoo~)lassen]

letter (mail) der Brief [dair breef] **>** 114

lie (untruth) die Lüge [dee luuguh]

lie down v sich hinlegen [zish hin-laygen]

life das Leben [dass lay-ben]

lifeboat das Rettungsboot [dass ret-ungss-boht] **>** 33

lift (Am: elevator) der Fahrstuhl [dair far-shtool]

light n das Licht [dass lisht];
adj hell [hel]; (weight) leicht [leisht]

lightning der Blitz [dair blits]

like v mögen [mer-gen]

line (Br: queue) die Reihe [dee rei-uh]

listen zuhören [tsoo-her-ren]

little klein [klein]; (a little) etwas [et-vass]; (a little bit of...) ein wenig von ... [ein vaynish fon]

live v leben [layben]; (reside) wohnen [vohnen]

located: to be located sich befinden [zish be-find-en]

location die Lage [dee lah-guh]

lock n das Schloss [dass shloss];
v zuschließen [tsoo-shlee-sen]

lodge (chalet) die Hütte [dee huu-tuh]

lone/lonely einsam [ein-zahm]

long adj lang [lang]

long-distance call das Ferngespräch
[dass fairn-ge-shpraysh] **>** 115

look schauen [show-en]; (look for) suchen [zoo-khen]

look after, take care of aufpassen (auf)
[owf-passen [owf]]

Look out! Vorsicht! [for-zisht]

lorry (Am: truck) der Lastwagen [dair lasst-vahgen]

lose verlieren [fair-leer-en] **>** 113

loss der Verlust [dair fair-lusst]

lost property office das Fundbüro
[dass funt-buuroh] **>** 113

lost: to get lost sich verirren [zish fair-ir-ren]

lot: a lot viel [feel]

loud laut [lowt]

loudspeaker der Lautsprecher [dair lowt-shpresh-er]

love v lieben [leeben]

low adj niedrig [need-rish], nieder [needer]

low season die Vorsaison [dee for-se-zoñ] **>** 72

luck n das Glück [dass gluuk];
lucky adj glücklich [gluuk-lish]

luggage (Am: baggage) das Gepäck [dass ge-pek]
> 30, 32

lunch das Mittagessen [dass mit-ahk-essen] **>** 40

████ **M** ████████████████████

machine die Maschine [dee mash-ee-nuh]

made from (material) aus [owss]

magazine die Zeitschrift [dee tseit-shrift] **>** 67

maiden name der Geburtsname
[dair ge-boorts-nahmuh] **>** 22

mail v (post) aufgeben [owf-gayben]

mainland das Festland [dass fesst-lant] **>** 33

make machen [makhen]; (to produce) herstellen
[hair-shtel-en]; (tea/coffee) (Kaffee/Tee) kochen
[(kafay/tay) kokhen]

make up one's mind sich entschließen
[zish ent-shlee-sen]

male/masculine männlich [men-lish]

man der Mann [dair man]

manager der Leiter [dair leiter],
die Leiterin [dee leiter-in]

map die Landkarte [dee lant-kartuh] **>** 67;
(of a town/city) der Stadtplan [dair shtat-plahn];
(walking/hiking) die Wanderkarte
[dee vander-kartuh] **>** 67, 88

market der Markt [dair markt] **>** 56, 81

marriage die Ehe [dee ay-uh]

married (to) verheiratet (mit) [fair-hei-rah-tet [mit]]

marry heiraten [hei-rah-ten]

mass (relig.) die Messe [dee messuh]

material der Stoff [dair shtof]

matter die Sache [dee zakhuh],
die Angelegenheit [dee an-ge-lay-gen-heit]

maybe vielleicht [fee-leisht]

me mich [mish]; (to me) mir [meer]

meal das Essen [dass essen],
die Mahlzeit [dee mahl-tseit];
(course, dish) das Gericht [dass ge-risht]

mean (signify) bedeuten [be-doyten]

measurements die Maße pl [dee mahss-uh];
das Maß sing [dass mahss]

meat das Fleisch [dass fleish] **>** 46, 48, 64

medicine das Medikament [dass may-dee-ka-ment]
> 57, 60, 107

meet begegnen [be-gayg-nen], treffen [tref-en]

memorise sich etw merken [zish et-vass mairk-en]

menu die Speisekarte [dee shpeize-kartuh] **>** 38, 46

message die Nachricht [dee nahkh-risht]

middle die Mitte [dee mit-uh]

minus minus [mee-nuss]

minute die Minute [dee mee-noo-tuh]

miss (someone, etc.) fehlen [faylen];
(a bus, etc.) verpassen [fair-passen]

Miss (title) das Fräulein [dass froy-lein]

mistake der Fehler [dair fayler];
(by mistake) aus Versehen [owss fair-zayen];
(to be mistaken) sich täuschen [zish toyshen]

misunderstand missverstehen [miss-fair-shtay-en]

mixed gemischt [ge-misht]

mobile phone (Am. cell phone) das Handy
[dass hendee] **>** 116

modern modern [moh-dairn]

moment der Augenblick [dair ow-gen-blik],
der Moment [dair moh-ment]

money Geld nt [gelt] **>** 106

month der Monat [dair moh-nat] **>** 18

moon der Mond [dair mohnt]

more mehr [mair]

morning der Morgen [dair morgen]; (in the mornings) morgens [morgenss], vormittags [for-mit-ahkss]

mosquito die Mücke [dee muu-kuh]

mother die Mutter [dee mut-er]

motive (reason, cause) der (Beweg~)Grund [dair (be-vayk~)grunt]

motor (engine) der Motor [dair mohtor] **>** 24, 27

motorbike das Motorrad [dass mohtor-raht] **>** 23

mountain der Berg [dair bairk]; (mountain range) das Gebirge [dass ge-bir-guh] **>** 82

move house umziehen [um-tsee-en]

movie der Film [dair film] **>** 83

Mr, Mrs Herr [hair], Frau [frow]

mud der Schmutz [dair shmuts]

museum das Museum [dass moo-zay-um] **>** 79, 80

music die Musik [dee moo-zeek]

my mein [mein]

■ N ■

naked nackt [nakt]

name der Name [dair nah-muh] **>** 11

nation die Nation [dee nat-see-ohn]

nationality die Staatsangehörigkeit [dee shtahts-an-ge-her-rish-keit]

natural natürlich [na-tuur-lish]

nature die Natur [dee na-toor]

nausea die Übelkeit [dee uubel-keit] **>** 111

near nahe [nah-he], bei [bei]; (nearby) in der Nähe [in dair nayuh]

necessary nötig [ner-tish]

need v benötigen [be-ner-ti-gen], brauchen [brow-khen]

neighbour der Nachbar [dair nakh-bar], die Nachbarin [dee nakh-bahr-in]

neither auch nicht [owkh nisht]

nephew der Neffe [dair nef-uh]

nervous nervös [nair-verss]

never nie [nee]; **nevertheless** trotzdem [trots-daym]

new neu [noy]

news die Nachrichten pl [dee nahkh-rish-ten]; (a piece of news) eine Neuigkeit [einuh noy-ish-keit]

newsagent's, news stand das Zeitungskiosk [dass tsei-tungss-kee-ossk]

newspaper die Zeitung [dee tsei-tung] **>** 67

next nächst [nay-ksst]; (next to) neben [nayben]

nice nett [net]

niece die Nichte [dee nish-tuh]

night die Nacht [dee nakht]; (spend the night) übernachten [uuber-nakh-ten] **>** 68

night club der Nachtclub [dair nakht-klup] **>** 82

nobody niemand [nee-mant]

noise der Lärm [dair lairm]

none/no kein [kein]

noon der Mittag [dair mit-ahk]; (at noon) zu Mittag [tsoo mit-ahk], mittags [mit-ahkss]

normal normal [nor-mahl]

north der Norden [dair norden]

North Sea die Nordsee [dee nort-zay]

not nicht [nisht]; (under no circumstances) keinesfalls [keiness-falss]; (not even) nicht einmal [nisht einmahl]

nothing nichts [nish-ts]

now jetzt [yetst], nun [noon]

nowhere nirgends [nirgents]

number die Nummer [dee num-er]; (figure) die Zahl [dee tsahl]; (phone) die (Telefon~)Nummer [dee (tay-lay-fohn~)num-er]

nurse der (Kranken~)Pfleger [dair (kranken~)pflay-ger], die (Kranken~)Pflegerin [dee (kranken~)pflay-ger-in]; (female only) die (Kranken~)Schwester [dee (kranken~)shvesster]

■ O ■

object der Gegenstand [dair gay-gen-shtant]

observe (the rules) beachten [be-akh-ten]

obtain erhalten [air-halten]

occasion die Gelegenheit [dee ge-laygen-heit]

occupied besetzt [be-zet-st]

ocean der Ozean [dair oh-tsay-ahn]

of von [fon]

of course natürlich [na-tuur-lish]

offend v beleidigen [be-lei-dig-en]

offer v anbieten [an-bee-ten]

office das Büro [dass buuroh]; (department) das Amt [dass amt]

often oft [oft]

oil das Öl [dass erl]

old alt [alt]

on prep auf [owf]

on the contrary! doch! [dokh]

once (one time) einmal [ein-mahl]

one (number) eins [einss]; (pronoun) man [man]

only nur [noor], lediglich [lay-dik-lish]

open v öffnen [erf-nen]; adj geöffnet [ge-erf-net]

opening hours die Öffnungszeiten [dee erf-nungss-tsei-ten]

opinion die Meinung [dee mein-ung]

opportunity die Gelegenheit [dee ge-la-gen-heit]

oppose: to be opposed to dagegen sein [da-gay-gen zein]

opposite n das Gegenteil [dass gay-gen-teil]; (location, etc.) entgegengesetzt [ent-gay-gen-ge-zet-st]

optician's der Optiker [dair op-tee-ker] **>** 56, 65

or oder [oh-der]

order die Bestellung [dee be-shtel-ung] **>** 38

organs: (internal) organs die (inneren) Organe [dee (in-er-en) or-gah-nuh]

origin die Herkunft [dee hair-kunft] **>** 14

other: the other der/die/das andere [dair/dee/dass an-der-uh]
our unser m/nt [unzer], unsere f [unzeruh]
out of order kaputt [ka-put]
outdoors im Freien [im frei-en]
outside außen [ow-sen], draußen [drow-sen]
oven der Ofen [dair oh-fen]
over über [uuber]
overseas Übersee [uuber-zay]
overtake überholen [uuber-hohlen]
owe schulden [shul-den]
own v besitzen [be-zit-sen]
owner der Besitzer [dair be-zit-ser], die Besitzerin [dee be-zit-ser-in]; der Eigentümer [dair eigen-tuumer], die Eigentümerin [dee eigen-tuumer-in]

P

pack v packen [pak-en]
package (small) das Päckchen [dass pek-shen]
page die (Buch~)Seite [dee [bookh~]zei-tuh]
pain der Schmerz [dair shmairts]
painting das Bild [dass bilt]
pair: a pair ein Paar nt [ine par]
papers (official documents) die Papiere nt, pl [dee pa-peer-uh] > 27, 118
parcel das Paket [dass pa-kayt] > 114
pardon: I beg your pardon? wie bitte? [vee bituh]
parents die Eltern [dee el-tern]
park n der Park [dair park]; v parken [parken] > 23
part (piece) das Teil [dass teil]
pass (mountain) der (Gebirgs~)Pass [dair (ge-birkss~)pass]
passage der Durchgang [dair doorsh-gang]
passenger der Passagier [dair passa-zjeer]
passing through (in transit) auf der Durchreise [owf dair doorsh-reizuh]
passport der (Reise~)Pass [dair (reizuh~)pass] > 22, 105
passport control die Passkontrolle [dee pass-kontrol-uh] > 22
past (go past) vorbei [for-bei]; (the past) die Vergangenheit [dee fair-gangen-heit]
path der Weg [dair vayk]
pay v bezahlen [be-tsah-len], zahlen [tsah-len]
pay duties/customs tax verzollen [fair-tsol-en]
pay v in cash bar zahlen [bar tsah-len]
payment die Zahlung [dee tsah-lung]
peace der Friede [dair free-duh]
people die Leute pl [dee loy-tuh]; (the people/ citizens) das Volk [dass folk]
per pro [proh]; **per cent** Prozent nt [proh-tsent]
percentage der Prozentsatz [dair proh-tsent-zats]
performance (theatre, etc.) die Vorstellung [dee for-shtel-ung] > 83
perhaps vielleicht [fee-leisht]
permission die Erlaubnis [dee air-lowp-niss]

person der Mensch [dair mensh], die Person [dee pair-zohn]
petrol (Am: gas) Benzin nt [ben-tseen] > 23
petrol station (Am: gas station) die Tankstelle [dee tank-shtel-uh] > 23, 27
pharmacy die Apotheke [dee a-poh-tay-kuh] > 57, 60
phone n das Telefon [dass tay-lay-fohn] > 115; v anrufen [an-roofen], telefonieren [tay-lay-foh-neer-en] > 115
phone call der Anruf [dair an-roof] > 115
photo das Foto [dass foh-toh]; **take a photo** fotografieren [foh-toh-graf-eer-en], knipsen [knip-sen] > 116
photographic equipment der Fotoartikel [dair fohtoh arteekel] > 56, 59
piece das Stück [dass shtuuk]
pillow das Kopfkissen [dass kopf-kissen]
pity: it's a pity es ist schade [ess isst shahduh]
place (location) die Stelle [dee shteluh], der Ort [dair ort]
plain (geog.) die Ebene [dee ay-ben-uh]
plant n die Pflanze [dee pflant-suh]
play v spielen [shpee-len]
please bitte [bituh] > 12
pleased (with) zufrieden (mit) [tsoo-freeden (mit)], **pleased (at)** erfreut (über) [air-froyt (uuber)]; **to be pleased (about)** sich freuen (über) [zish froyen (uuber)]
pleasure das Vergnügen [dass fairg-nuugen]
plus plus [pluss]
poison das Gift [dass gift]
poisoning die Vergiftung [dee fair-gif-tung] > 111
police die Polizei [dee poh-leets-ei] > 117
polite höflich [herf-lish]
politics die Politik [dee poh-lee-teek]
poor (not rich) arm [arm]
port (harbour) der Hafen [dair hah-fen] > 33
position (location) die Stellung [dee shtelung], die Lage [dee lah-guh]; (job) die Stelle [dee shteluh],
possible möglich [merklish]
post office das Postamt [dass posst-amt] > 56, 114
post v (mail) aufgeben [owf-gayben]
postpone verschieben [fair-shee-ben]
pot (for cooking) der (Koch~)Topf [dair (kokh~)topf]
pottery die Töpferwaren [dee terp-fer-var-en], die Keramik [dee kair-ah-mik]
prayer das Gebet [dass ge-bayt]
prefer vorziehen [for-tsee-en]
pregnant schwanger [shvanger]
prescribe verschreiben [fair-shrei-ben] > 108
present (gift) das Geschenk [dass ge-shenk]
present: to be present da sein [dah zein]
pretty adj hübsch [huupsh]
price der Preis [dair preiss]
priest der Priester [dair pree-ster], die Priesterin [dee pree-ster-in]

DICTIONARY

prison das Gefängnis [dass ge-feng-niss] **> 118**
prize der Preis [dair preiss]
probable/probably wahrscheinlich [var-shein-lish]
profession der Beruf [dair be-roof]
programme (Am: program) das Programm [dass proh-gram] **> 83**; (Radio/TV programme) die (Radio~/ Fernseh~)Sendung [dee rah-dee-oh~/ fairn-zay~]zen-dung]; (theatre) der Spielplan [dair shpeel-plahn]
promise das Versprechen [dass fair-shpresh-en]
pronounce v aussprechen [owss-shpresh-en]
protection der Schutz [dair shuts]
public öffentlich [er-fent-lish]
public holiday der Feiertag [dair fei-er-tahk] **> 18**
public transport der Nahverkehr [dair nah-fair-kair] **> 34**
pull ziehen [tsee-en]
punishment die Strafe [dee shtrah-fuh]
purchase n der Kauf [dair kowf]
purse der Geldbeutel [dair gelt-boytel]
push stoßen [shtoh-sen]
put (place) stellen [shtelen], setzen [zet-sen]; (put down) legen [laygen]

Q

quality die Qualität [dee kva-lee-tayt]; (characteristic) die Eigenschaft [dee eigen-shaft]
question die Frage [dee frahguh]
queue (Am: line) die Reihe [dee rei-uh]
quick/quickly schnell [shnel], rasch [rash]
quiet/quietly ruhig [roo-ish], still [shtil]
quite ganz [gants]

R

radio das Radio [dass rah-dee-oh]
railway line die (Bahn~)Strecke [dee (bahn~]shtrekuh]
railway/railroad die Eisenbahn [dee eizen-bahn] **> 31**
rain regnen [rayg-nen]
ramp die Rampe [dee rampuh]
rape n die Vergewaltigung [dee fair-ge-val-ti-gung] **> 117**
rare/rarely selten [zelten]
rather lieber [leeber]
reach erreichen [air-reish-en]
read lesen [layzen]
ready fertig [fair-tish]
realize erkennen [air-ken-en]
reason n der Grund [dair grunt], die Ursache [dee oor-zakh-uh]
receipt die Empfangsbestätigung [dee emp-fangss-be-shtay-ti-gung]
receipt: make a receipt quittieren [kvit-eer-en]
receive erhalten [air-halten]
recent adj kürzlich [kuurts-lish]; **recently** adv kürzlich [kuurts-lish], neulich [noy-lish]

reception der Empfang [dair emp-fang]; (hotel) die Rezeption [dee ray-tsep-tsee-ohn] **> 69**
recognize erkennen [air-ken-en]
recommend empfehlen [emp-fay-len]
recover (after illness, etc.) sich erholen [zish air-hoh-len]
red rot [roht]
reduction die Ermäßigung [dee air-may-si-gung] **> 32**
refuse v ablehnen [ap-lay-nen], sich weigern [zish vei-gern]
region die Gegend [dee gay-gent]
register v (baggage) aufgeben [owf-gay-ben] **> 31**
registration die Anmeldung [dee an-mel-dung]
related (family) verwandt [fair-vant]
reluctantly ungern [un-gairn]
remedy das (Heil~)Mittel [dass [heil~]mit-el] **> 60**
remember sich erinnern [zish air-in-ern]
remind s.o. of sth jdn an etw erinnern [yay-man-den an et-vass air-in-ern]
rent die Miete [dee mee-tuh] **> 74**
rental car der Mietwagen [dair meet-vahgen] **> 29**
repair n die Reparatur [dee ray-pa-ra-toor]; v reparieren [ray-pa-ree-ren], wiederherstellen [vee-der-hair-shtel-len]
repeat wiederholen [veeder-hoh-len]
replace ersetzen [air-zet-sen]
replacement der (Schaden~)Ersatz [dair (shahden~]air-zats]
reply n die Antwort [dee ant-vort]; v antworten [ant-vor-ten], beantworten [be-ant-vor-ten]
request n die Bitte [dee bituh] **> 12**
reservation die Buchung [dee bookh-ung], die Reservierung [dee ray-zair-veer-ung] **> 72**
residence (place of) der Wohnort [dair vohn-ort], der Wohnsitz [dair vohn-zits] **> 23**
responsible verantwortlich [fair-ant-vort-lish]
rest n (a break) eine Pause [einuh pow-zuh]; (the rest) der Rest [dair resst]
restaurant das Restaurant [dass ress-toh-rañ] **> 36**
restless unruhig [un-roo-ish]
result das Ergebnis [dass air-gayp-niss]
return n die Rückkehr [dee ruuk-kair]; v wiederkommen [vee-der-kom-en]
ribbon das Band [dass bant]
rich (money) reich [reish]
right adj richtig [rish-tish]; n (entitlement) das Recht [dass resht]; (to be right) Recht haben [resht hahben]
right: on the right rechts [reshts]
ring (doorbell, etc.) klingeln [kling-eln]
risk n das Risiko [dass ree-zee-koh]
river der Fluss [dair fluss], der Strom [dair shtrohm]; (riverbank) das (Fluß~)Ufer [dass (fluss~]oof-er]
road map die Straßenkarte [dee shtrah-sen-kartuh] **> 28**

road sign der Wegweiser [dair vayk-vei-zer]

rock n der Fels [dair felss]

room das Zimmer [dass tsim-er], der Raum [dair rowm]; (bedroom) das (Schlaf~)Zimmer [dass (shlahf~)tsim-er]; (space) der Platz [dair plats]

rotten faul [fowl]

round adj rund [runt]

route die Route [dee rootuh], der Weg [dair vayk]

rubbish (Am: garbage) der Müll [dair muul]

rule die Regel [dee raygel], die Vorschrift [dee for-shrift]

run (on foot) laufen [low-fen]

S

sad traurig [trow-rish]; (sadness) der Kummer [dair kum-er], die Trauer [dee trow-er]

safety pin die Sicherheitsnadel [dee zisher-heits-nahdel]

sale der Verkauf [dair fair-kowf]

same gleich [gleish]; (the same) der/die/das gleiche [dair/dee/dass gleishuh]; (one and the same thing) ein und dasselbe [ein unt dass-zel-buh]

satisfied zufrieden [tsoo-free-den]

sausage die Wurst [dee voorst] > 48

save (a life, etc.) retten [ret-en]

say v sagen [zahgen]

scorpion der Skorpion [dair skor-pee-ohn]

Scotland Schottland [shot-lant]

Scots(~man/~woman) der Schotte [dair shot-uh], die Schottin [dee shot-in]

sea das Meer [dass mair], die See [dee zay]

season die Jahreszeit [dee yah-ress-tseit], die Saison [dee se-zoñ] > 18

seat der (Sitz~)Platz [dair (zits~)plats]

second (unit of time) die Sekunde [dee zay-kun-duh]

secret/secretly geheim [ge-heim]; (in secret) heimlich [heim-lish]

security die Sicherheit [dee zisher-heit]

see sehen [zayen]; (see again) wiedersehen [vee-der-zayen]

self-service shop/store der Selbstbedienungsladen [dair zelpsst-be-dee-nungss-lahden]

send schicken [shik-en], senden [zenden]

sender (package, etc.) der Absender [dair ap-zender] > 114

sentence (phrase) der Satz [dair zats]

separate adj getrennt [ge-trent]

serious ernst [airnsst]

serve v servieren [zair-veer-en]

service (relig.) der Gottesdienst [dair go-tess-deensst] > 80; (restaurant) die Bedienung [dee be-dee-nung]

service/rest station (motorway/highway) die Raststätte [dee rasst-shte-tuh]

settle (a matter) erledigen [air-lay-di-gen]

severe (illness, etc.) schwer [shvair]

sex Sex m [sekss]

shade (colour) der (Farb~)Ton [dair (farp~)tohn]

shades (Br: sunglasses) die Sonnenbrille [dee zon-en-bril-uh]

shameless (impertinent) unverschämt [un-fair-shaymt]

she sie [zee]

ship das Schiff [dass shif] > 33

shoe der Schuh [dair shoo]

shop (Am: store) das Geschäft [dass ge-sheft], der Laden [dair lahden] > 54

shop: to go shopping einkaufen gehen [ein-kow-fen gayen] > 54

shore (sea) das (Meeres~)Ufer [dass (mair-ess~)oof-er]

short kurz [kurts]; (person) klein [klein]

shortage der Mangel [dair man-gel]

shot (gun, etc.) der Schuss [dair shuss]

shout schreien [shrei-en]

show zeigen [tsei-gen]

shut schließen [shlee-sen], zumachen [tsoo-makhen]

shy schüchtern [shuush-tern]

sick (Br. ill) krank [krank] > 110

side die Seite [dee zei-tuh]

sights (tourism) die Sehenswürdigkeiten [dee zayens-vuur-dish-keit-en] > 79

sightseeing tour of a town/city die Stadtrundfahrt [dee shtat-runt-fart] > 79, 81

sign n das Schild [dass shilt]

signature die Unterschrift [dee unter-shrift] > 106

silence das Schweigen [dass shvei-gen], die Ruhe [dee roo-uh], die Stille [dee shtil-uh]; (silently) schweigend [shvei-gent]

since (time) seit [zeit]; (since when?) seit wann? [zeit van]; (because) da [dah]

sing singen [zin-gen]

single (relationship status) ledig [lay-dish] > 23

sister die Schwester [dee shvess-ter]

sister-in-law die Schwägerin [dee shvay-ger-in]

sit sitzen [zit-sen]; (sit down) sich setzen [zish zet-sen], sich hinsetzen [zish hin-zet-sen]

situated: to be situated liegen [leegen]

situation die Lage [dee lahguh]

size die Größe [dee grer-suh]

sky der Himmel [dair him-el]

sleep v schlafen [shlah-fen]

slim (thin) schlank [shlank]

slow/slowly langsam [lang-zahm]

small klein [klein]

small talk der Smalltalk [dair smorl-tork] > 13

smell n der Geruch [dair ge-rukh]; v riechen [ree-shen]

smoke rauchen [row-khen]

smoker der Raucher [dair row-kher], die Raucherin [dee row-kher-in]

smuggle schmuggeln [shmug-eln]

snack der Imbiss [dair im-biss];

snack bar die Imbissbude [dee im-biss-boo-duh]

snow v schneien [shnei-en]

so, thus   also [al-zoh]
society   die Gesellschaft [dee ge-zel-shaft]
soft   weich [veish]
solid (firm)   fest [fesst]
some   einige [ei-ni-guh]
somebody   jemand [yay-mant]
something   etwas [et-vass]
sometimes   manchmal [mansh-mahl]
son   der Sohn [dair zohn]
song   das Lied [dass leet]
soon   bald [balt]
sort (kind)   die Art [dee art]
sort out   regeln [ray-geln]
source   (information) die Quelle [dee kve-luh];
   (water) die Quelle [dee kve-luh]
south   der Süden [dair zuu-den]
souvenir   das Souvenir [dass soo-ven-eer] ➤ 66
space   der Raum [dair rowm]
speak   sprechen [shpresh-en]
speed   die Geschwindigkeit [dee ge-shvin-dish-keit]
spell v   buchstabieren [bookh-shta-beer-en]
spoiled (ruined)   verdorben [fair-dor-ben]
spoon   der Löffel [dair ler-fel]
sport   der Sport [dair shport] ➤ 84
sports field   der Sportplatz [dair shport-plats]
square (town/city, etc.)   der (Markt~)Platz
   [dair (markt~)plats] ➤ 81
staff   das Personal [dass pair-zohn-ahl]
stairs, staircase   die Treppe [dee trep-uh]
stamp   n Briefmarke [dee breef-markuh];
   v (e.g. a ticket) frankieren [fran-keer-en] ➤ 114;
stand   stehen [shtayen]
star   der Stern [dair shtairn]
start   beginnen [be-gin-en]
state n   (condition) die Verfassung [dee fair-fass-ung];
   (nation) der Staat [dair shtaht]
station   der Bahnhof [dair bahn-hohf] ➤ 31
stationery   Schreibwaren pl [shreip-vahren] ➤ 67
stay   n der Aufenthalt [dair ow-fent-halt];
   v bleiben [blei-ben]
steal   stehlen [shtaylen]
steep   steil [shteil]
still (e.g. still more)   noch [nokh]
sting v   stechen [shtesh-en]
stone   der Stein [dair shtein]
stop   v aufhören [owf-her-ren]; (an~)halten
   [(an~)hal-ten]; n (bus stop, etc.) die Haltestelle
   [dee hal-tess-shteluh] ➤ 34
stop!   halt! [halt]; (stop it!) hör auf ! [her owf]
stopover/layover   der Zwischenstopp
   [dair tsvish-en-shtop] ➤ 31
store (Br: shop)   das Geschäft [dass ge-sheft],
   der Laden [dair lahden] ➤ 54
storm   das Gewitter [dass ge-vit-er]
story (tale)   die Geschichte [dee ge-shish-tuh]
stove   der Ofen [dair oh-fen]

straight on   geradeaus [ge-rah-duh-owss]
stranger   der/die Fremde [dair/dee frem-duh]
street (road)   die Straße [dee shtrah-suh]
study v   studieren [shtoo-deer-en]
stupid   dumm [dum]
style   der Stil [dair shteel]
suburb   der Vorort [dair for-ort],
   die Vorstadt [dee for-shtat]
subway   die Unterführung [dee unter-fuur-ung]
success   der Erfolg [dair air-folk]
sudden/suddenly   plötzlich [plerts-lish]
suitcase   der Koffer [dair kof-er]
sum (math.)   die Summe [dee zum-uh]
summit   der Gipfel [dair gip-fel];
   (fig.) der Höhepunkt [dair her-punkt]
sun   die Sonne [dee zon-uh]; (sunny) sonnig [zon-ish]
sunglasses (Am: shades)   die Sonnenbrille
   [dee zon-en-bril-uh]
supermarket   der Supermarkt [dair zooper-markt]
supplement n   Zuschlag m [tsoo-shlahk] ➤ 32
sure/surely   sicher [zisher]
surname   der Familienname
   [dair fam-ee-lee-en-nah-muh] ➤ 23
surprised   überrascht [uuber-rasht]
swear v   schimpfen [shimp-fen],
   fluchen [floo-khen]
sweat v   schwitzen [shvit-sen]
swim v   schwimmen [shvim-en] ➤ 84
swimming pool   das Schwimmbad [dass shvim-baht]
switch: (light~)switch n   der (Licht~)Schalter
   [dair (lisht~)shalter]
sympathy (condolences)   das Beileid [dass bei-leit]

T

table   der Tisch [dair tish]
take   nehmen [naymen]; (take with) mitnehmen
   [mit-naymen]; (transport) bringen [bringen];
   (s.o. somewhere) mitnehmen [mit-naymen]
take part in   teilnehmen an [teil-nay-men an]
take place   stattfinden [shtat-finden]
take-off   der Abflug [dair ap-flook] ➤ 29
talk v   reden [ray-den]
tall   groß [grohss]
taste   n der Geschmack [dair ge-shmak];
   v schmecken [shmek-en], probieren [proh-beeren]
tax   die Steuer [dee shtoyer]
taxi   das Taxi [dass tak-see] ➤ 35
telephone n   das Telefon [dass tay-lay-fohn] ➤ 115
telephone line   die Verbindung [dee fair-bin-dung]
tell v   erzählen [air-tsay-len]
temperature   die Temperatur
   [dee tem-per-a-toor] ➤ 19
terrible   fürchterlich [fuursh-ter-lish],
   schrecklich [shrek-lish]
than (comparison)   (for differences) als [alss];
   (for similarities) wie [vee]

thanks danke [dankuh]; **thank (s.o.)** (jdn) danken [(yay-man-den) dank-en] **>** 12

that's why deshalb [dess-halp]

theatre das Theater [dass tay-ah-ter] **>** 83

theft der Diebstahl [dair deep-shtahl] **>** 117

their ihr [eer]

then (next, later, afterwards) dann [dan]; (at that time) da [dah]; (back then, in the past) damals [dah-mahlss];

there dort [dort], da [dah]; (over there) da drüben [dah druu-ben];

therefore daher [da-hair]

they sie [zee]

thin dünn [duun]

thing das Ding [dass ding], die Sache [dee zakhuh]

think (about) v denken (an) [denken (an)]; (opinion) meinen [meinen]

thirsty: to be thirsty durstig sein [durss-tish zein]

this/these (this) diese/r/s f/m/nt [deezuh/zair/zess]; (these) diese [deezuh]

that/those (that) jene/r/s f/m/nt [yaynuh/nair/ness]; (those) jene [yaynuh]

thought der Gedanke [dair ge-dank-uh]

through prep durch [doorsh]

ticket (travel) die Fahrkarte [dee far-kartuh] **>** 34; (event, museum, etc.) die (Eintritts~)Karte [dee (ein-trits~)kartuh]

ticket office (event) die Kasse [dee kassuh]; (travel) der Fahrkartenschalter [dair far-kar-ten-shal-ter]; (box office) die Theaterkasse [dee tay-ah-ter-kassuh]

time die Zeit [dee tseit] **>** 16; (time of day) die Uhrzeit [dee oor-tseit]; (one time) ein Mal [ein mahl]; (on time) rechtzeitig [resht-seit-ish], pünktlich [puunkt-lish]

timetable der Fahrplan [dair far-plahn] **>** 32

tip (Am: gratuity) das Trinkgeld [dass trink-gelt] **>** 35, 40

tired müde [muu-duh]

tiring anstrengend [an-shtren-gent]

to (in direction of) zu [tsoo]; (to London) nach London [nahkh lon-don]

tobacco der Tabak [dair tab-ak]

today heute [hoy-tuh]

together zusammen [tsoo-za-men]

toilet die Toilette [dee twa-let-uh] **>** 32, 70, 72, 118

tolerate, put up with ertragen [air-trah-gen]

tomorrow der Morgen [dair mor-gen]

tone (sound) der Ton [dair tohn]

too much/many zu viel [tsoo feel]

topic (of a conversation, etc.) das (Gesprächs~) Thema [dass (ge-shpray-shss~)tay-mah]

tour die Besichtigung [dee be-zish-tigung] **>** 78

tourist information office das Verkehrsamt [dass fair-kair-zamt]

tow (away) abschleppen [ap-shlep-en] **>** 28

towards (direction) gegen [gaygen]

town die Stadt [dee shtat]

town centre die Innenstadt [dee in-en-shtat]

town hall das Rathaus [dass raht-howss] **>** 80

toy das Spielzeug [dass shpeel-tsoyk]

traffic n der Verkehr [dair fair-kair]

train der Zug [dair tsook] **>** 31

transfer v (money) überweisen [uuber-veizen]

transit visa das Durchreisevisum [dass doorsh-reizuh-vee-zum]

translate übersetzen [uuber-zet-sen]

travel agency das Reisebüro [dass reize-buu-roh]

travel v reisen [reizen]

traveller's cheque/check der Reisescheck [dair reize-shek] **>** 106

tree der Baum [dair bowm]

trip n der Ausflug [dair owss-flook] **>** 81

truck (Br: lorry) der Lastwagen [dair lasst-vahgen]

true wahr [var]

try v versuchen [fair-zookhen]

tunnel n der Tunnel [dair tun-el]

typical (of) typisch (für) [tuup-ish (fuur)]

U

ugly hässlich [hess-lish]

umbrella der Schirm [dair shirm]

uncertain unsicher [un-zish-er], ungewiss [un-ge-viss]

uncle der Onkel [dair on-kel]

unconscious (out cold) bewusstlos [be-vusst-lohss], ohnmächtig [ohn-mesh-tish] **>** 113

under unter [unter]

underground (railway) die U-Bahn [dee oo-bahn] **>** 35

understand verstehen [fair-shtayen]

underway (in transit) unterwegs [unter-vaykss]

uneasy unwohl [un-vohl]

unfortunately leider [lei-der]

unfriendly unfreundlich [un-froynt-lish]

unhappy unglücklich [un-gluuk-lish]

unhealthy ungesund [un-ge-zunt]

United States Amerika [a-mair-ee-kah]; die Vereinigte Staaten (von Amerika) [dee fair-ein-ish-tuh-shtah-ten (fon a-mair-ee-kah)]

unknown fremd [fremt], unbekannt [un-be-kant]

unlucky unglücklich [un-gluuk-lish]

until bis [biss]

up prep oben [ohben]

urgent dringend [dring-ent]

us, to us uns [unss]

use v benutzen [be-nut-sen]

V

vacant (bathroom, etc.) frei [frei]

vacation die Ferien [dee fairee-en], der Urlaub [dair oor-lowp]

DICTIONARY

vain: in vain umsonst [um-zonsst], vergeblich [fair-gayp-lish]
valid gültig [guul-tish] ➤ 22
value der Wert [dair vairt]
vegetables das Gemüse [dass ge-muu-zuh] ➤ 41, 49, 64
versus gegen [gaygen]
very sehr [zair]
view n (sight) die Aussicht [dee owss-zisht]; (opinion) die Ansicht [dee an-zisht], die Meinung [dee mei-nung]
village das Dorf [dass dorf], die Ortschaft [dee ort-shaft]
visa das Visum [dass vee-zum]
visible sichtbar [zisht-bar]
visit n der Besuch [dair be-zookh]; v besuchen [be-zookhen], besichtigen [be-zish-ti-gen]
voice die Stimme [dee shti-muh]
volume (book) der Band [dair bant]
vote v wählen [vay-len]

W

wage (salary) der Lohn [dair lohn]
wait for warten auf [varten owf]
waiter/waitress der Kellner [dair kelner], die Kellnerin [dee kelner-in]
waiting room (doctor's, etc.) das Wartezimmer [dass vartuh-tsim-er]; (railway station, etc.) der Wartesaal [dair vartuh-zahl]
wake v wecken [vek-en]
Wales Wales [way-elss]
walk v gehen [gayen]; (to go for a walk) spazieren gehen [shpat-see-ren gayen]
wallet die Brieftasche [dee breef-tashuh] ➤ 117
want v wollen [vol-en], wünschen [vuunsh-en]
war n der Krieg [dair kreek]
warm adj warm [varm]
warn (about) warnen (vor) [varnen (for)]
warning! achtung! [akh-tung]
wash v waschen [vash-en]
watch v zuschauen [tsoo-show-en]; n (wristwatch) die Armbanduhr [dee arm-bant-oor]
water das Wasser [dass vasser]; (drinking water) das Trinkwasser [dass trink-vasser]
way (of doing sth) die Art [dee art]; (route) der Weg [dair vayk]
we wir [veer]
weak schwach [shvakh]
wear v tragen [trah-gen]
weather das Wetter [dass vet-er] ➤ 19
web address die Internetadresse [dee internet-ad-ress-uh] ➤ 8
wedding die Hochzeit [dee hokh-tseit]
week die Woche [deevokhuh] ➤ 17
weigh v wiegen [vee-gen]
weight das Gewicht [dass ge-visht]

welcome! willkommen! [vil-kom-en]
well... (interjection) nun ... [noon]
well adj gut [goot]
west der Westen [dair vess-ten]
wet nass [nass], feucht [foysht]
what? was? [vass]
wheelchair der Rollstuhl [dair rol-shtool]
when wenn [ven]; (when?) wann? [van]; (describing past event) als [alss]
where? wo? [voh]; (where from?) Woher? [voh-hair]; (where to?) Wohin? [voh-hin]
whether ob [op]
which welche/r/s f/m/nt [vel-sh-uh/-er/-ess]
while während [vay-rent]
white weiß [veiss]
who? Wer? [vair]; (whom?) Wen? [vayn]; (to whom?) Wem? [vaym]
whose? Wessen? [vessen]
why? Warum? [va-rum]
wide breit [breit], weit [veit]
wife die (Ehe~)Frau [dee (ay-uh~)frow]
win v gewinnen [ge-vin-en]
wish v wünschen [vuun-shen]
with mit [mit]
within (time) innerhalb [in-er-halp]
without ohne [oh-nuh]
witness der Zeuge [dair tsoy-guh], die Zeugin [dee tsoy-gin]
woman die Frau [dee frow]
wood (timber) das Holz [dass holts]
word das Wort [dass vort]
work v arbeiten [ar-bei-ten]; (function) funktionieren [funk-tsee-on-neer-en]
working days werktags [vairk-tahkss]; sing der Werktag [dair vairk-tahk]
workshop die Werkstatt [dee vairk-shtat] ➤ 24, 27
world die Welt [dee velt]
worry n die Sorge [dee zorguh]; v (to worry about) sich sorgen [zish zorgen], sich Sorgen machen [zish zorgen makhen]
worth: to be worth a lot viel wert sein [feel vairt zein]
write v schreiben [shrei-ben]
writing: in writing schriftlich [shrift-lish]
wrong falsch [falsh]; (to be wrong) sich irren [zish ir-ren]

Y

year das Jahr [dass yar]
yellow gelb [gelp]
you sing/inf du [doo]; pl/inf ihr [eer]; pl/formal Sie [zee]
young jung [yung]
your sing/inf dein [dein]; pl/inf euer [oy-er]; pl/formal Ihr [eer]
youth hostel die Jugendherberge [dee yoo-gent-hair-bair-guh]

> DOS & DON'TS

Wait for the Green Man!

Whatever you do in Germany, make sure you don't cross the road until the Green Man says you can! Even if there isn't a car in sight, you'll find people patiently waiting at the side of the road until the striding green figure makes his appearance. If you don't, you can be fined by the police or (even worse!) be told off by an irate parent for setting a bad example to their kids.

Just Friends...?

If you refer to someone as *mein Freund/meine Freundin* [mein froynd/mein-uh froynd-in], people will assume that they're your boyfriend or girlfriend. If your relationship's merely platonic, make sure to refer to your companion as *ein Freund/eine Freundin von mir* [ein froynd/einuh froynd-in fon meer] ("a friend of mine").

Denglish Dos and Don'ts

Denglish – a mix of Deutsch and English – is taking the German-speaking world by storm. People are having fun mixing up English with their native tongue, and the results are weird, wonderful, and often downright confusing for native English speakers! Some of the words – like *Handy* [hendee] ("mobile/cell phone") and *Beamer* [bee-mer] ("projector") – are ingenious new creations that won't give you any trouble at all. Other words – like a *Smoking* ("a tuxedo or dinner jacket") – have changed their meanings, but

shouldn't cause you any major headaches. Occasionally, however, you'll come across some *Denglish* vocab that might make you want to run a mile! But don't worry: if someone offers you a *Bodybag* [bodee-bag], they're not suggesting your days are numbered (it's a type of over-the-shoulder messenger bag). And if you're approached by a *Streetworker* [street-verker], don't panic – you've not necessarily strayed into the seedy side of town (they're a kind of social worker!).

With Friends Like These...

German and English are quite closely related. This can be helpful as it allows you to understand some words with no problem at all (e.g. Finger, Fisch, Gold, etc.). But watch out – there are some words lurking in the language that almost seem designed to trip you up! A *Rathaus* [rat-howss], for instance, isn't home to legions of rodents (it's a town hall), you won't get a good work out at a *Gymnasium* [guum-nah-zee-um] (it's a type of school), and avoid buying your loved one a *Gift* [gift] ("poison").

Seven Deadly Sins?

If someone asks you a question starting with the words *Hast du Lust ...* [hasst doo lusst] (lit: "do you have 'lust'..."), don't get over excited. Although *Lust* can refer to one of the more passionate deadly sins, in this context it just means "Would you like/Would you fancy" (i.e. *Hast du Lust mitzukommen?* [hasst doo lusst mit-tsoo-kom-en] – "Would you like to come with us?").